STUDIES IN A DYING CULTURE

AAKAR BOOKS CLASSICS

STUDIES IN A DYING CULTURE

Christopher Caudwell

Introduction by
John Strachey

AAKAR

STUDIES IN A DYING CULTURE
Christopher Caudwell

First Aakar Edition 2017

ISBN 978-93-5002-515-4

Published by
AAKAR BOOKS
28 E Pocket IV, Mayur Vihar Phase I
Delhi 110 091, India
aakarbooks@gmail.com
www.aakarbooks.com

Printed at
Sapra Brother, Delhi 110 092

INTRODUCTION

'YOU know how I feel about the importance of democratic freedom. The Spanish People's Army needs help badly; their struggle, if they fail, will certainly be ours to-morrow, and, believing as I do, it seems clear where my duty lies.'

The author of this book gave the above explanation for enlisting in the British Battalion of the International Brigade, which he did on December 11th, 1936.

On February 12th, 1937, he was holding a hill above the Jarama River, as one of a machine-gun section under the command of a Dalston busman. That afternoon he was killed.

'. . . What I feel about the importance of democratic freedom.' Now Caudwell was a Communist. And many people sincerely suppose that Communists are the dangerous enemies of democratic freedom; they believe that if Communists declare their attachment to democracy, or to freedom, they are only doing so in order to deceive. Yet here we have a Communist, not merely declaring his attachment to democracy and freedom; not merely declaring, as Mr. Neville Chamberlain has recently done, for example, his readiness to die in defence of democracy, but, in actual fact, dying for democracy.

Surely there is something to puzzle over here? Do

men fight and die for a political manœuvre? Do they face the Fascist assault; do they face the onrush of the new barbarism armed with every device of infernal science; do they face that charge, made by war-maddened Moorish Tribesmen, supported by the perfected products of German and Italian aviation which killed Caudwell; do they leave home to face all that, for the sake of a democratic freedom in which they do not really believe?[1] And yet Caudwell was a Communist; a Communist who died for democratic freedom.

The Elizabethans said that death was eloquent. Perhaps the death of Caudwell, and of the men from London and Glasgow and Middlesbrough and Cardiff who have died with him in Spain, may so speak that

[1] Here is an extract from an eye-witness account of his death: 'On the first day Sprigg's' (Caudwell was a literary pseudonym) 'section was holding a position on a hill-crest. They got it rather badly from all ways, first artillery, then machine-gunned by aeroplanes, and then by ground machine-guns. The Moors then attacked the hill in large numbers and as there were only a few of our fellows left, including Sprigg, who had been doing great work with his machine-gun, the company commander, ——, the Dalston busman, gave the order to retire.

'Later I got into touch with one of the section who had been wounded while retiring, and he told me that the last they saw of Sprigg was that he was covering their retreat with the advancing Moors less than thirty yards away. He never left that hill alive, and if any man ever sacrificed his life that his comrades might live, that man was Sprigg.'

the people of Britain will begin to understand why Communists fight and die for democratic freedom; for it seems that nothing less than the indubitable signature of death will make men believe in their sincerity.

Caudwell, however, did more than die for his beliefs. For twenty-nine years he lived for them. And into these years he packed a remarkable amount of activity. He wrote a quite startling number of books. For instance, he wrote, under his real name of Christopher St. John Sprigg, no less than seven detective stories (I have read one of them and thought it very poor, as a matter of fact), five books on aviation, and a great number of short stories and poems.

And these were merely his pot-boilers. For the work he really cared about he reserved the pseudonym of Caudwell. Above this name he wrote a serious novel called *This My Hand* (which, in my view, is a failure) and three major works, namely, *Illusion and Reality*, *The Crisis in Physics* and the present volume.

We catch the impression of a young man possessed by creative energy; a young man turning out a flood of work, good, bad and indifferent; a young man, however, marked with one of the most characteristic and one of the rarest of the signs of promise, namely, real copiousness. He was a young man who not only warmed his hands before, but gave great hearty pokes at, the fire of life; a young man so interested in everything, from aviation, to poetry, to detective stories, to quantum mechanics, to Hegel's philosophy, to love, to psycho-analysis, that he felt that he had simply got to say something about them all.

That is what a man in his 'twenties ought to be like. It is true that such a man isn't very likely to say anything conclusive about aviation, love or quantum mechanics.[1] When such a man is about thirty years old, however, his omnivorous attention will settle upon the intensive study of one, or perhaps two, chosen fields; and it will be incomparably the richer for its wandering decade.

Caudwell was just twenty-nine, he was finding himself; his last books show a sharp gain in precision, in capacity to focus; and then the Moors came.

It is not my purpose to say anything of his two other considerable works, *Illusion and Reality* and *The Crisis in Physics.* The single purpose of this introduction is to proclaim the unity between the theme which runs through every one of the eight studies of this book and the cause for which its author died; to proclaim the exquisite unity between Caudwell's theory and his practice; the unity which is, I suppose, what people mean when they talk about sincerity.

For this book is about Liberty. It is a sustained, complex, elaborate, vehement attempt to explain what liberty is, why Communists fight and die for it, and

[1] The extraordinary thing is that Professor Levy says that Caudwell did say some extremely significant things about physics.

why they know that in the final analysis Communism is Liberty.

The book takes the form of a number of essays on such contemporary figures as Shaw, T. E. Lawrence, D. H. Lawrence, Wells and Freud, with a paper on pacifism, and another on love, and a summing up on liberty itself, thrown in. Such a diversity of subjects might be expected to make the book scrappy and disconnected; but it has not done so. Almost every page is knit together by a central and never forgotten theme, namely, the analysis, from every angle, of the concept of human liberty. The method which Caudwell chose, that of exemplifying his theme by studies of some of the more influential contemporary minds, makes the book rich and concrete where it might easily have become meagre and abstract.

Caudwell's introductory chapter gives out his theme. By universal admission something is wrong with contemporary culture. In spite of the enormous achievements of twentieth-century science, everyone feels that the whole vast body of culture, of which science, art, religion, and philosophy are component parts, is rotting. Yet, no one can diagnose the disease. 'What is the explanation?' Caudwell writes:

'Either the Devil has come amongst us having great power, or there is a causal explanation for a disease common to economics, science and art. Why then have not all the psycho-analysts, Eddingtons, Keynes, Spenglers, and bishops who have surveyed the scene, been able to locate a source of infection common to all modern culture, and, therefore, surely obvious enough? For answer, these people must take to themselves the words of Herzen: " We are not the doctors, we are the disease." '

Caudwell's answer is given by the whole of the rest of his book, but he attempts to sum it up both in the introductory chapter and in his last essay on liberty. His answer is that the men of to-day, the men who determine the mental climate of our epoch, have profoundly mistaken the nature of human liberty. As the achievement of liberty is, explicitly or implicitly, the universal goal for which all men work, a mistake about the very nature of liberty vitiates all our endeavours from the very outset. In a few sentences (but to state the idea in a few sentences is to mutilate and to impoverish it) the leaders of contemporary culture are still dominated, whether they know it or not, with the Rousseauesque belief that man was born free but has enslaved himself in a net of social relations; that the freest man is the most isolated; that what we have to do in order to regain the liberty of the 'natural man' is to unloose all the coercions and ties of society; to dissolve the community into its original elements again.

Caudwell's theme, to which he returns again and again, is that this conception is the prime error which is at the root of all our confusions. This wholly negative conception of liberty had its justification when the task before mankind was the striking off of feudal fetters, the dissolution of a rigid outworn system of social relations within which the powers of mankind were cabined. Then it was true, relatively and temporally, that the dissolution of an obsolete set of social relations, by which men consciously dominated each other, was the task of the liberator. To-day this old truth has died and its corpse has become the most pestilence-breeding of errors.

It is not that we do not still need to seek liberty as the highest of all human ends.

'There are many essays of Bertrand Russell,' Caudwell writes, 'in which this philosopher explains the importance of liberty, how the enjoyment of liberty is the highest and most important goal of man. Fisher claims that the history of Europe during the last two or three centuries is simply the struggle for liberty. Continually and variously, by artists, scientists, and philosophers alike, liberty is thus praised and man's right to enjoy it imperiously asserted.

'I agree with this. Liberty does seem to me the most important of all generalised goods—such as justice, beauty, truth—that come so easily to our lips.'

But the achievement of liberty to-day depends on a process opposite to that undertaken by the anti-feudal liberators. It is not a question to-day of dissolving conscious, overt, feudal bonds by which one man, or class of men, is dominating another. The task of the twentieth-century liberator is, on the contrary, a treble one.

First his analytic task is to make conscious the contemporary, unconscious, unseen social bonds and compulsions which have grown up in the society which resulted from the work of the men, and the class, which destroyed feudalism. This side of the twentieth-century liberators' task is to make men conscious of the fact that when they, rightly, destroyed the overt feudal bond of serf to lord, and slave to slave-owner, they, all unknowingly, wove new, subtle, invisible bonds of domination. Of these the bond between the employer and the employee is the type; and these bonds have become, for all their intangibility, more cruel and coercive in many respects, than the old, overt bonds of servitude.

This tragic result was inevitable because of a profound though, perhaps, historically necessary contradiction in the conception of the goal towards which the anti-feudal—the liberal—liberators were working. Because they thought that the freest man was the most isolated; because, as Caudwell points out, the beast of the jungle is the ultimate ideal of freedom for the liberal who has taken liberalism to its ultimate conclusion; because they did not see that when they destroyed the putrescent connective tissue of the feudal body politic, they must perforce evolve some new social connective tissue to take its place, they neglected the whole constructive side of their task.

But their omission did not mean that new social

relations were not established. That would have been impossible ; that would have meant the dissolution of human society. It simply meant that the new, post-feudal, social relations, under which we still live, were established unconsciously. These are the social relations of capitalism, the social relations of the market. Every man is now free, none has legal, compulsive powers over any other. Society is composed of free atoms.

But how are these human atoms to meet at all? How are men to organise any form of co-operation for associated labour? How are social interconnections of any kind to be achieved? The answer is that new and tighter, though now unconscious and invisible, bonds have grown up behind men's backs out of those commercial relations of buying and selling which were the one form of social intercourse allowed in the theory of post-feudal society. This single relation of buying and selling, by turning into the relation of buying and selling men's power to labour, has become the compulsive relation of employer to employee ; it has become an acute form of domination. In modern society almost the only relation of which men are conscious is their relation to the commodities which they buy and sell. But behind this relation to things has lain concealed a social relation ; a relation of domination to other men. To make all this conscious ; to make men realise that they live in a highly, though invisibly, intergraded society, is the first, analytic step of the work of the modern liberator.

The second step is to make men realise that all that is good in capitalist society ; that everything in which it shows its superiority to feudal society, arises, by a supreme historical paradox, from the higher degree of integration, the richer growth of social connective tissue, which the new form of society has unconsciously produced ; that everything which is bad in capitalist society ; the subservience of man to man ; the extreme and ever-growing instability of the whole system ; its slumps and its wars, and its present disintegration, arises because of the unconscious and, therefore, uncontrolled and uncomprehended nature of these new, close and dominating social relations.

The third and highest task of the contemporary liberator is to make men realise that they will find liberty, first, by breaking down, it is true, the existing, unconscious, set of social relations and coercions. But then, if they are to be free, they must build up new, conscious, rich, close and complex social relations ; they must build up those social relations which we call socialism. Somehow we must make men understand that they can find liberty, not in the jungle, which is the most miserably coercive place in the world, but in the highest possible degree of social co-operation. Liberty is a positive and not a negative concept ; liberty is the presence of opportunity rather than the absence of constraint ; liberty is the ability to do what we want. And that we cannot do, upon this obstinate earth, except in close, conscious and organised co-operation with our fellow-men.

These few sentences maim and constrict Caudwell's exposition of the concept of liberty as a positive social relation ; the concept of liberty as the attainment of the highest degree of mutual aid. The reader of this book will find this concept diversely illustrated and illuminated in almost every one of its pages.

Again, it has been to misrepresent Caudwell's book to suggest that it is simply an essay on liberty. It is true that this theme runs through it ; that this theme is what gives it unity and singleness of purpose. But there are many other suggestive and stimulating themes in the book. Caudwell makes a real contribution, for example, to the study of Freudian psychology as a social phenomenon. Again he has some amusing and shrewd things to say about Wells and Shaw.

Indeed the particular essay which interested me most was that on T. E. Lawrence. In it, Caudwell develops what I can only call a theory of heroism. He asks the question, what is a hero ? Why did the huge convulsion of the world war produce no hero in that part of the world which stayed within the confines of capitalist society ? Why does Lenin, the man who burst those confines for one great people, alone stand out to save our epoch from incomparable mediocrity ? He answers this question by a study of the nearest thing to a hero which the British ruling class was able to produce, the hero *manqué*, T. E. Lawrence.

There is profound understanding and sympathy in

Caudwell's study of this supremely original, supremely unhappy, genius. This essay, above all perhaps, makes us feel how profound has been our loss through the death of Caudwell. In this essay Caudwell shows a capacity which is as yet tragically rare amongst the writers, and leaders, of the British working-class movement. He shows a width of perception, a generosity of sympathy, a capacity to understand the motive forces which move the minds of men. He shows an ability to use his Marxian insight into impersonal social forces in order to gain an understanding of the tragedies of individual men.

Well, because we were too lazy, too selfish, too frightened to see to it that our country played its part in preventing the world from becoming the playground of the Fascist aggressors, Caudwell has been killed ; and many another such, who might have lived to bless the world, will be killed. Let us, at least, use the words which Caudwell did have the opportunity to leave us, to make all those who are becoming men and women in the blood-stained nineteen-thirties understand for what it was he died.

JOHN STRACHEY.

FOREWORD

'We are living in a very singular moment of history. It is a moment of crisis, in the literal sense of that word. In every branch of our spiritual and material civilisation we seem to have arrived at a critical turning-point. This spirit shows itself not only in the actual state of public affairs but also in the general attitude towards fundamental values in personal and social life.

'. . . Formerly it was only religion, especially in its doctrinal and moral systems, that was the object of sceptical attack. Then the iconoclast began to shatter the ideals and principles that had hitherto been accepted in the province of art. Now he has invaded the temple of science. There is scarcely a scientific axiom that is not nowadays denied by somebody. And at the same time almost any nonsensical theory that may be put forward in the name of science would be almost sure to find believers and disciples somewhere or other.'

MAX PLANCK : 'WHERE IS SCIENCE GOING ?' 1933.

AS the above quotation shows, one does not have to be a Marxist to declare that bourgeois culture is seriously ill. In art, science, religion, economics and ethics, there is dissension, and a thousand confessions of bewilderment and pessimism could be drawn from the writings of the acknowledged leaders of contemporary culture from Einstein to Freud. All the old easy confidence of a century ago has evaporated. The only consolation religion has is that science disavows causality; and scientists draw comfort from the fact that 'practical' men are unable to run the ship of state anywhere but on the rocks.

Yet bourgeois culture during the last fifty years has achieved much. Its empirical developments include relativity and quantum physics, genetics, a new insight into the deeper layers of man's mind, the different patterns of social relationships uncovered by anthropology, and hundreds of technicological inventions such as the aeroplane, wireless, motor transport, and electric power. Why, with this proved record, does it despair?

It despairs because each discovery is like a Midas touch, which prepares a new disappointment. Quantum physics appears to have withdrawn reality from the domain of science by denying causality. The psychological discoveries have produced a hopeless confusion in which hundreds of radically different psychological schools struggle for leadership. Bourgeois anthropology claims to have shown that the stability of societies rests on illusion. But modern man has no illusions—or believes he has none. And the unparalleled increase in productive powers has given birth, not to peace, plenty, and happiness, but to war, famine, and misery. Anarchy is the keynote of the crisis in all spheres. The crisis has this characteristic of anarchy, that though all men will one thing to be the result of their efforts, what is brought about by them is precisely the opposite. And it has this further characteristic of anarchy, that the more men wish to gain a common truth, a common faith, a common world-view, the more their efforts at ideological construction increase the sum of contradictory and partial views of reality.

What is the explanation? Either the Devil has come amongst us having great power, or there is a causal explanation for a disease common to economics, science, and art. Why then have not all the psychoanalysts, Eddingtons, Keynes, Spenglers, and bishops who have surveyed the scene, been able to locate a source of infection common to all modern culture, and, therefore, surely obvious enough? For answer, these people must take to themselves the words of Herzen: 'We are not the doctors, we are the disease.'

The Marxist's first task is to separate, from this confusion, the elements that represent real empirical discoveries, and fit them into his synthetic world-view. This is comparatively easy. More laborious is the analysis of the cause which, in each discovery, makes it go bad, so to speak, upon the inventor's hands. Why does this strange doom hang over bourgeois culture, that its progress seems only to hasten its decay? And how can one cause operate in so many different fields, and bring about so many different forms of decay and confusion?

These Studies are concerned with both tasks, synthetic and analytic, but the second is regarded as at this stage more important and valuable. Some of them may seem unduly critical in tone for a work with the quoted words of Lenin at its forefront. But the critical approach to bourgeois culture has this value, that it is always the application of the same method. In art, philosophy, physics, psychology, history, sociology, and biology the 'crisis' of bourgeois culture is always due to the same cause. And this is no accident, because that destructive illness was originally the dynamic force of bourgeois civilisation ; but now, its utmost potentialities accomplished, it is a power for ill. Worn-out engines become brakes. Outworn truths become illusions. Bourgeois culture is dying of a myth.

But it will be said, bourgeois culture is suffering not from illusion but from disillusionment. Everyone has said it—Freud, Jung, D. H. Lawrence, and the Archbishop of Canterbury. Precisely, for this is the very danger of its illusion, that it believes itself disillusioned. It has shed all the secondary illusions—of religion, God, morality, democracy, teleology, and metaphysics. But it cannot rid itself of the basic bourgeois illusion, and because it is unaware of this illusion, and because this illusion is now stripped to its naked essence, it violently distorts the whole fabric of contemporary ideology.

This illusion is that man is naturally free—'naturally' in this sense, that all the organisations of society are held to limit and cripple his free instincts, and furnish restraints which he must endure and minimise as best he may. From which it follows that man is at his best and noblest when freely working out his own desires.

This illusion is of course the Renaissance charter of the *bourgeoisie*. It claimed for the 'natural man' freedom from all feudal restrictions, privileges, and monopolies. The basic relation of society was to be freedom from any relation—the free merchant, the free labourer, and free capital. With each man thus freely following his desires, the best interests of society as a whole would, it was asserted, be served. This principle, superior to the feudal principle, made the bourgeois class supreme and dynamic and, for a time, gave this principle the sanction of eternal truth. And it is still the assumption on which bourgeois culture is based.

If it were true, all would be well. It would be fine if freedom were as easy as this, that man was naturally free. But it is not true. Freedom is the product, not of the instincts, but of social relations themselves. Freedom is secreted in the relation of man to man. This demand of bourgeois culture was in fact unrealisable. Man cannot strip himself of his social relations and remain man. But he can shut his eyes to these social relations. He can disguise them as relations to commodities, to the impersonal market, to cash, to capital, and his relations then seem to have become possessive. He 'owns' the commodities, the cash and the capital. All his social relations appear to have become relations to a thing, and because man is superior to a thing, he is now free, he is dominating. But this is an illusion. By shutting his eyes to all the relations between men that constitute society, and are its real stuff and substance, man has enslaved himself to forces whose control is now beyond him, because he does not acknowledge their existence. He is at the mercy of the market, the movement of capital, and the slump and boom. He is deluded by himself. This is shown by the remorseless test of events.

This bourgeois freedom of each man struggling for his free desires and his own profit, so far from making us free, has long delivered us over, bound to chance. Blind Fate, in the shapes of war, unemployment, slumps, despair and neurosis, attacks the 'free' bourgeois and his 'free' followers. His struggles put him into the power of finance capital, trustify him, or, if he is a 'free' labourer, he is herded into the mass-production factory. So far from being free, he is whirled like a leaf on the gales of social change. And all this anarchy, and impotence, and muddled dissension is reflected in his culture. Productive forces have outgrown the free bourgeois, and mercilessly crush him and his illusions.

Can such a simple error, if it be an error, infect the cool realms of physics, the remote spheres of art, and the inner world of psychology? Can it distort philosophy and hold back the hero from success? How can it appear everywhere in ideology, always as the distorting factor, without being observed as such? But it is just because it appears everywhere in his ideology, like the Fitzgerald contraction, in measurements of ether velocity, that it cannot be observed by the bourgeois, any more than the physicist can observe the earth's speed through the ether.

These 'Studies in a Dying Culture' are varied though their subjects may be united by the one theme. This theme is the lie at the heart of contemporary culture, the lie which is killing it; and deeper still is found the truth which is the complement to this lie, the truth which will transform and revitalise culture.

CONTENTS

STUDIES IN A DYING CULTURE

I

GEORGE BERNARD SHAW

A STUDY OF THE BOURGEOIS SUPERMAN

'*A good man fallen among Fabians.*' LENIN

SHAW in his life acquired general recognition among the ordinary members of the 'middle class' both here and in America, as representative of Socialist thought. The case of Shaw is in many ways interesting and significant; is a proof of how stubborn is the bourgeois illusion. The bourgeois may be familiar with Marxism and keenly critical of the social system, and anxious to change it, and yet all this leads only to an ineffectual beating of the air because he believes that man is in himself free.

Shaw is an ex-anarchist, a vegetarian, a Fabian, and, of late years, a Social Fascist: he is inevitably an *Utopian* socialist. His idea of Utopia was expounded in *Back to Methuselah*, a paradise of Ancients who spend their days in *thought* and despise the butterfly young who engage in the *active* work of artistic creation and science.

Shaw then exposed the weakness as well as the essence of his characteristically bourgeois brand of socialism. It represents the primacy of pure contemplation. In pure contemplation man is alone, is apparently exempt from co-operation, is wrapped in a private world ; and he is then believed, by bourgeois thought, to be wholly free. Is not this the illusion of the scientist ? No, for science is not *pure* thought, it is thought allied to action, testing all its cogitations at the bar of reality. It is thought as thought ought to be, passing always in dialectic movement between knowing and being, between dream and outer reality. Shaw abhors this kind of thought. He abhors modern science not as he might do for its human weaknesses, but hating it for its essence, for its social qualities, for all that is good in its active creative rôle.

This is a familiar spectacle : the intellectual attempting to dominate hostile reality by 'pure' thought. It is a human weakness to believe that by retiring into his imagination man can elicit categories or magical spells which will enable him to subjugate reality contemplatively. It is the error of the 'theoretical' man, of the prophet, of the mystic, of the metaphysician, in its pathological form the error of the neurotic. It is the trace of the primitive believer in magic that remains in us all. In Shaw it takes a characteristically bourgeois form. He sees that truth brings freedom, but he refuses to see that this understanding is a social product and not a thing that one clever man can find alone. Shaw still believes that out of his Platonic soul man can extract pure wisdom in the form of world-dominating Ideas, and out of debate and ratiocination, without social action, beat out a new and higher consciousness.

It is notable that the real artist, like the real scientist, never makes this mistake. Both find themselves repeatedly pushed into contact with reality; they desire and seek reality outside them.

Reality is a large, tough, and—as man gets to know it—increasingly complex substance. To know it requires the socially pooled labours of generations of men. So complex has science already grown that a man can only hope to grasp completely a small corner of it. The old dream of all-knowledge for one mind has vanished. Men must be content to co-operate by giving a few stitches in the vast tapestry, and even these few stitches may be as complex as the earlier large design of a Newton or a Darwin.

Now Shaw with his bourgeois individualism is impatient at the restriction science sets on the domination of reality by one acute intellect. Shaw cannot hope to master the apparatus of science, therefore he sweeps it all away as mumbo-jumbo. It is nonsense, Shaw says, that the sun is ninety million miles away from the earth. Natural Selection is preposterous. And so instead of these concepts reached with so much labour, Shaw puts forward ideas drawn purely from his desires like those of any Hindoo mystic theorising about the world. Sweeping aside all science as nonsense, he rewrites the history of reality in terms of a witch-doctor's 'life-force' and a jam-to-morrow God. Shavian cosmology is barbarous; it is idealistic.

Shaw dominates this tough, distressing, gritty environment by the familiar neurotic method, by imposing on it a series of fictional delusions of a wish-fulfilment type. This is not because Shaw is foolish but precisely because he is possessed of a naturally acute intellect. Its very acuteness has given him a pride which makes him feel he ought to be able to dominate all knowledge without social aid, by pure cerebration. He will not recognise, except cursorily, the social nature of knowledge. So we get in his cosmology an effect like that of an exceptionally brilliant medicine man theorising about life. Since the average intellectual is still infected with similarly barbaric theorising, it is not surprising that he does not detect the essential crudity of all Shaw's philosophy. Bourgeois speaks to bourgeois.

It is barbarous to believe in action without thought, that is the Fascist heresy. But it is equally barbarous to believe in thought without action, the bourgeois intellectual heresy. Thought is immobilised—or rather races like a machine with nothing to bite on—once it is declutched from action, for thought is an aid to action. Thought guides action, but it learns *how* to guide *from* action. Being must historically and always proceed knowing, for knowing evolves as an extension of being.

Shaw's instinctive bourgeois belief in the primacy of lonely thought is of course evidenced not only in his ludicrous cosmology and repulsive Utopia, but also in his Butlerian biology, in which the various animals decide whether they want long necks and so forth, and by concentrating their minds on this aim, succeed in growing them. Ludicrous as this Butlerian neo-Lamarckianism is, it has enormous emotional influence on the bourgeois mind. It appeals to it so powerfully that sober scientists, even while admitting that no atom of evidence can be found for this hypothesis and all kinds of evidence for the opposite standpoint, yet insist on giving it a provisional approval, because it seems so 'nice' to them. To a mind obsessed with bourgeois concepts of liberty and the autonomy of the individual mind, such a conception seems to promise a kind of substitute for the paradise which determinism denies him.

This would be unimportant if Shaw's Fabianism did not pervade all his work, robbing it of artistic as well as of political value. Believing in the solitary primacy of thought, all his plays are devoid of humanity, because they represent human beings as walking intellects. Fortunately they are not, or the human race would long ago have perished in some dream-fantasy of logic and metaphysics. Human beings are mountains of unconscious being, walking the old grooves of instinct and simple life, with a kind of occasional phosphorescence of consciousness at the summit. And this conscious phosphorescence derives its value and its power from the emotions, from the instincts ; only its form is derived from the intellectual shapes of thought. Age by age man strives to make this consciousness more intense, the artist by subtilising and intensifying the emotions, the scientist by making fuller and more real the thought form, and in both cases this is done by burning more being in the thin flame. Shaw, however, is obsessed with the 'pure' flame, phosphorescence separate from being. The ideas thus abstracted become empty and petty and strike with a remote tinkling sound in the ears. Shaw's plays become an 'unearthly ballet of bloodless categories'.

This mixed thought and feeling of consciousness is not the source of social power, only a component of it. Society with its workshops, its buildings, its material solidity, is always present below real being and is a kind of vast reservoir of the unknown, unconscious and irrational in every man, so that of everyone we can say his conscious life is only a fitful gleam on the mass of his whole existence. Moreover, there is a kind of carapacious toughness about the conscious part of society which resists change, even while, below these generalisations, changes in material and technique and real detailed being are going on. This gives rise in every man to a tension which is a real dynamic force in society, producing artists, poets, prophets, madmen, neurotics and all the little uncertainties, irrationalities, impulses, sudden unreasoning emotions, all the delights and horrors, everything that makes life the thing it is, enrapturing the artist and terrifying the neurotic. It is the sum of the uneasy, the anti-conservative, the revolutionary. It is everything which cannot be content with the present but causes lovers to tire of love, children to flee their happy parental circle, men to waste themselves in apparently useless effort.

This source of all happiness and woe is the disparity between man's being and man's consciousness, which drives on society and makes life vital. Now all this tension, everything below the dead intellectual sphere, is blotted out in Shaw. The Life Love, which is his crude theological substitute for this real active being, is itself intellectually conceived. Thus his characters are inhuman ; all their conflicts occur on the rational plane, and none of their conflicts are ever resolved—for how can logic ever resolve its eternal antimonies, which can only be synthesised in action ? This tension creates ' heroes ' like Cæsar and Joan of Arc, who, in response to the unformulated guidance of experience, call into existence tremendous talent forces of whose nature they can know nothing, yet history itself seems to obey them. Such heroes are inconceivable to Shaw. He is bound to suppose that all they brought about they consciously willed. Hence these heroes appear to him as the neat little figures of a bourgeois history book, quite inhuman, and regarding their lives as calmly as if they were examination papers on the ' currents of social change '. These plays are not dramas. This is not art, it is mere debate and just as unresolved, just as lacking in tragic finality, temporal progress or artistic unity as is all debate.

For this reason, too, Shaw is a kind of intellectual aristocrat, and no one who is not capable of declaring his motives rationally and with the utmost acuity on instant demand appears in his plays, except as a ludicrous or second-rate figure. The actors are nothing ; the thinkers are everything. Even a man who in real life would be powerful, formidable and quite brainless —the 'armourer' of 'Major Barbara'—has to be transformed into a brilliant theoretician before (as Shaw thinks) he can be made impressive on the stage. But we all know and admire characters devoid of the ability for intellectual formulation who yet seem in their influence upon reality nobler, grander, more powerful and effective than any of our intellectual friends. We know well enough in life at all events, that thought alone does not suffice to drive on the world, and recognise this in our homage to 'illusory' 'irrational' art, art that speaks to the mere experience of us, stirring it into a fleeting and purely emotional consciousness ? None of these characters, who in war, art, statesmanship and ethics have been of significance in the world's history, appear in Shaw's plays. He is incapable of drawing a character who is impressive without being a good arguer in bourgeois dialectic. This weakness naturally shows itself in his proletarians. Like the proletarians in the Army hostel of Major Barbara, they are simply caricatures. Only by being 'educated', like the chauffeur in *Man and Superman*, can they become respectable.

It therefore follows that Shaw's ideal world is a world not of communism, but like Wells' is a world ruled by intellectual Samurai guiding the poor muddled workers; a world of Fascism. For bourgeois intellectuals obsessed with a false notion of the nature of liberty are by the inherent contradictions of their notion at length driven to liberty's opposite, Fascism. Shaw's Utopia is a planned world imposed from above in which the organisation is in the hands of a bureaucracy of intellectuals. Such a world is negated by the world of communism, in which all participate in ruling and active intellectuals, no longer divorced from being, learn from the conscious worker just as much as the workers demand guidance from thought. The fatal class gap between thought and action is bridged. This world, with its replaceable officials not specially trained for the task, is the opposite of the old Fabian dream or nightmare, the class Utopia in which the ruling class now takes the form of a permanent, intellectual, trained bureaucracy, wielding the powers of State for the 'good' of the proletariat. This world was a pleasant dream of the middle class, which neither owned the world, like the capitalist, nor had the certainty of one day owning it like the proletariat. It is an unrealisable dream which yet holds the intellectual away from the proletariat and makes him a bulwark of reaction and Fascism. Shaw is still obsessed with the idea of liberty as a kind of medicine which a man of goodwill can impose on the 'ignorant' worker from without. That liberty would be medicine for the bourgeois, not the worker. He does not see that neither intellectual nor worker possesses as yet this priceless freedom to give, both are confined within the categories of their time, and communism is the active creation of true liberty which cannot yet be given by anybody to anybody. It is a voyage of discovery, but we are certain of one thing. The liberty which the Roman, the feudal lord and the bourgeois achieved, proved illusory, simply because they believed that a ruling class could find it, and impose it on society. But we can see that they failed and man is still everywhere in chains, because they did not share the pursuit of liberty with their slaves, their serfs, or the exploited proletariat; and they did not do so because to have done so would have been to cease to be a ruling class, a thing impossible until productive forces had developed to a stage where ruling classes were no longer necessary. Therefore, before the well-meaning intellectual, such as Shaw, seeks this difficult liberty, he must first help to change the system of social relations to one in which all men and not a class have the reins of society in their hands. To achieve liberty a man must govern himself; but since he lives in society, and society lives by and in its productive relations, this means that for men to achieve liberty society must govern its productive relations. For a man to rule himself presupposes that society is not ruled by a class from which he himself is excluded. The search for liberty only begins in the classless state, when society, being completely self-governing, can learn the difficult ways of freedom. But how can this be achieved when its destiny is planned by a class, or controlled by the higgling of a market, or even arranged by a company of elegant Samurai? How can the intellectual Samurai ever agree, since no two philosophers have ever agreed about absolute truth and justice? Only one referee has ever been found for the interminable *sic et mon* of thought—action. But in a world where thought rules and action must hold its tongue, how can the issue ever be resolved? Action permeates every pore of society: its life is the action of every man. Society is torn apart as soon as its form is determined by the thought of a few which is privileged and separate from the action of the many.

Since Shaw implicitly denies the elementary truth that thought flows from being, and that man changes his consciousness by changing his social relations, which change is the result of the pressure of real being below those relations. Shaw must necessarily deny the efficacy of revolutionary action as compared with the activities of propaganda. Like Wells he believes that preaching alone will move the world. But the world moves, and though it moves through and with preaching, it does not follow that all preaching moves it, but only that that preaching moves it which moves with the law of motion of the world, which marches along the line of action, and cuts down the grain of events. Yet a bourgeois intellectual always believes that whatever he conceives as absolute truth and justice —vegetarianism or equal incomes or anti-vaccination —can be imposed on the world by successful argument. Hence Shaw's plays.

But here Shaw is faced with a dilemma. He is to impose his absolute truths on the world by the process of logical debate. But the world of non-thinkers or half-thinkers on which he imposes it are necessarily an inferior race of creatures—the mere labourers, the nit-wit aggregation of the non-intellectuals, the plastic amorphous mass whom the intellectual lords of creation save from disaster by their god-like commands. How can one drill sense into these creatures? What will appeal to their infantile frivolous minds? One must of course treat them as one treats children, one must sugar the pill of reason with paradox, humour, with lively and preposterous incident.

Thus Shaw, whom a belief in the primacy of intellectual consciousness prevented from becoming an artist, was by this same belief prevented from becoming a serious thinker or a real force in contemporary consciousness. He became the world's buffoon; because his messages were always wrapped in the sugar of humour, they were taken as always laughable. The British bourgeois, who ignored Marx, vilified Lenin and threw its Tom Manns into prison, regarded Shaw with a tolerant good-humour as a kind of court jester. The people he had depreciated depreciated him. The sugar he put on his pill prevented the pill from acting.

Marx by contrast did not attempt to make *Das Kapital* appealing to the tired brains of the British bourgeoisie. He did not attempt to become a best-seller, or veil his views in West End successes. He did not give humorous interviews to the contemporary press. His name was known only to a few Englishmen of his time, while that of Shaw is known to millions. But because he gave his message seriously, treating the race of men as his equals, his message was received seriously and well. Because he did not believe that thought rules the world, but that thought must follow the grain of action, his thought has been more world-creating than that of any single man. Not only has it called into existence a new civilisation over a sixth of the world's surface, but in all other countries all revolutionary elements are oriented round Marx's thought ; all contemporary politics are of significance only in so far as they are with Marx or against him.

It is no answer to say that Marx's is a greater intellect than Shaw's. Doubtless if Shaw had been Marx he would have been Marx. No one has devised a standard for measuring intellects in themselves, since intellects do not exist in themselves, but only in their overt mentation. Shaw and Marx were both men of keen intellect, as evidenced in their writings, and both were aware, from experience, of the breakdown of greedy bourgeois social relations ; but the mind of one was able to leap forward to the future, the other is prisoned always in the categories of the bourgeoisdom it despises. Because Shaw gave his message condescendingly and flippantly, treating the race of men as his inferiors, his message has been much read and little noted, and the message itself betrays all the falsehood and unreality of the attitude which settled its delivery.

Shaw read Marx early in life, and he was given therefore the alternative of being a dangerous revolutionary instead of a popular reformist who would dream of a world saved by a converted middle-class. He decided that although Marx had shown him the shame and falsities of bourgeois life, he would refuse to recognise the necessity for the overthrow of this decaying class by the class of the future. From that moment Shaw was divided against himself.

This decision is explained by his personal history. Born into a middle-class family that had fallen from affluence and social position to embarrassment, the ambitious young Shaw, impressed from childhood with the necessity for retrieving the former Shavian status, came to London to gain success. Here he existed for a time by writing, as poor as any worker. But thanks to the possession of a dress-suit and a gift for playing on the piano, he was still able to mix in refined Kensington circles. Faced with proletarianisation, he clung to the bourgeois class. In the same way, faced with the problem of ideological proletarianisation in his reading of Marx, he resisted it, and adhered to Fabianism, with its bourgeois traditions and its social respectability.

This problem and his answer to it, decided his ideology and also his art. His knowledge of Marx enabled him to attack destructively all bourgeois institutions. But he was never able to give any answer to the question : *What shall we do here and now to improve them besides talking ?* This problem, in the veiled form of ' tainted money ', comes up in his work repeatedly —in *Widower's Houses, Major Barbara, Mrs. Warren's Profession*—and always it is *patched up.* We must accept things as they are until the system is changed. But no immediate steps besides talking, are ever to be taken to change the system. Major Barbara, horrified at first by finding the Christ she believes in has sold out to capital, ends all the same by marrying the manager of the armament factory whose proprietor has bought Him. Shaw himself, who discovered the ruling class was rotten to the core, and built on the exploitation of the workers, yet ends by marrying ideologically money, respectability, fame, peaceful reformism and ultimately even Mussolini. He who takes no active steps to change the system, helps to maintain the system.

Yet just because Shaw has read Marx, he understands the essential contradictions of this solution. For this reason his plays are full of deliberately forced conversions, unconvicing *dénouements*, and a general escape from reality through the medium of fantasy and humour. Shaw dealt quite simply in his life with the problem of tainted goods that arose from the sufferings of animals. Meat and sera, one resulting from the slaughter and the other from the vivisection of animals, must not be used, even though in spite of one's abstention the wicked business goes merrily on. But he cannot make that renouncement in the case of money and of all the intangibles of bourgeois respectability—fame as a Fabian intellectual instead of suppression as a dangerous revolutionary. Meat and sera are not essential to the life of society, and therefore it is possible to abstain from them. In bourgeois society money is what holds society together: no one can ever eat without it; therefore it is impossible to 'abstain' from it. But this in itself exposes the futility of Shaw's bourgeois abstaining approach to the problem, like that of the pacifist who will not fight but continues to be fed at the expense of the community. Shaw's ambivalent attitude to social evils reveals his cowardice before the prime evil, the very hinge of society, which he will accept, while he abstains from the lesser evils. Thus his vegetarianism acts as a kind of compensation for his betrayal on the larger issue, and a symbol of his whole reformist approach. He will abstain; he will criticise; but he will not act. This last refusal infects his criticism and makes his abstention an active weapon of reaction. And so, all through his plays and prefaces, money is the god, without which we are nothing, are powerless and helpless. 'Get money, and you can be virtuous; without it you cannot even start to be good.' Shaw repeats this so often and so loudly that he seems anxious to convince himself as well as others. 'Renounce it,' he asks, 'and what help is your altruism? Even if you throw it in the gutter, some scoundrel will pick it up. Wait till the system is changed.'

But how is it to be changed? Shaw has no convincing answer. There is no need to accuse Shaw of conscious dishonesty. Shaw is helplessly imprisoned in the categories of bourgeois thought. He could not see, that because being conditions knowing, the bourgeois class for all their 'cleverness' are doomed to collapse and the workers for all their 'stupidity' are able to play an active creative rôle in building a new civilisation on the wreckage of the old. Faced with this choice—*worker or bourgeois*—the bourgeois—with all the brilliance of bourgeois culture behind him—seemed to Shaw preferable to the other, ignorant, 'irrational' and 'brutalised' by poverty. Hence arose his life problem, how to persuade this bourgeois class to renounce its sins. He had to convert them, or fold his hands in despair ; and yet in his heart he did not believe in their future, for he had read Marx.

This decision, conditioned by his class and his experience, led to all his difficulties. He could never really bring himself to believe in a bourgeois class regenerated by Fabianism, and events made still clearer its hopelessness and its decay. Hence, more and more, his plays become futile and unresolved. Civilisation is driven 'On the Rocks' or is in the 'Apple Cart'. Relief is found in the faith of a Life Force making inevitably for a Utopia (*Back to Methuselah*). Or as in *St. Joan* he tries to comfort himself by turning to a period when this class he has committed himself to, this bourgeois class, played an active creative part : he draws St. Joan as the heroine and prophet of bourgeois individuality, amid a dying medievalism. In

Heartbreak House he records simply a Tchekovian detachment and disillusion. Evidently all Shaw's failing, all the things that prevented him from fulfilling the artistic and intellectual promise of his native gifts, arise in a most direct fashion from his fatal choice of the bourgeois class at a period of history when the choice was wrong. From this choice springs the unreality of his plays, their lack of dramatic resolutions, the substitution of debate for dialectic, the belief in life forces and thought Utopias, the bungling treatment of human beings in love, the lack of scientific knowledge, and the queer strain of mountebank in all Shaw says, as of a man who in mocking others is also mocking himself because he despises himself but despises others more.

Shaw performed a useful function in exposing the weakness of the bourgeois class. He exposes the rottenness of its culture and at the same time commits the future to its hands, but neither he nor his readers can believe in the success of that ; and so he represents symbolically bourgeois intelligence as it is to-day, shamefaced and losing confidence in itself. He plays this active part, that he is one of the forces of defeatism and despair which help the decay of a world that has had its day. This disintegration is no more than pathological without the active forces of revolution which can shatter the rotten structure and build it anew. This confidence Shaw has never achieved, nor the insight that is needed for it. He stands by the side of Wells, Lawrence, Proust, Huxley, Russell,

Forster, Wassermann, Hemingway, and Galsworthy as typical of their age, men who proclaim the disillusionment of bourgeois culture with itself, men themselves disillusioned and yet not able to wish for anything better or gain any closer grasp of this bourgeois culture whose pursuit of liberty and individualism led men into the mire. Always it is their freedom they are defending. This makes them pathetic rather than tragic figures, for they are helpless, not because of overwhelming circumstances but because of their own illusion.

II

T. E. LAWRENCE

A STUDY IN HEROISM

ALTHOUGH the leading powers of the world directed during the four years of the Great War all their material, scientific, and emotional resources to violent action, this unprecedented struggle produced no bourgeois master of action. The Great War had no hero. On the other hand, the Russian Revolution was guided from the start by Lenin, who has since grown steadily in significance, not only in Soviet Russia, but throughout the bourgeois world. Whereever there is a social ferment, the actions and words of Lenin are part of it ; and each year makes clearer the fact that, as on a hinge, twentieth-century history turns on Lenin. Hindenburg, Ludendorff, Joffre, Jellicoe, French, Haig, Foch, Lloyd George, Wilson and Grey are figures which grow more and more ludicrous and petty as they recede down the tide of time. In the twentieth century millions of deaths and mountains of guns, tanks and ships are not enough to make a bourgeois hero. The best they achieved was a might-have-been, the pathetic figure of T. E. Lawrence.

Yet, if any culture produced heroes, it should surely be bourgeois culture? For the hero is an outstanding individual, and bourgeoisdom is the creed of individualism. The bourgeois age was inaugurated by a race of hero giants; the Elizabethan adventurers and New World conquistadors loom largely out of the rabble of history. The bourgeois progress gives us Cromwell, Marlborough, Luther, Queen Elizabeth, Wellington, Pitt, Napoleon, Gustavus Adolphus, George Washington. Indeed bourgeois history, for bourgeois schools, is simply the struggles of heroes with their antagonists and difficulties.

What is it that constitutes heroism? Personality? No; men with the flattest and simplest personalities have become heroes. Is it courage? A man can do no more than risk and perhaps lose his life, and millions did that in the Great War. Is it success—the utilisation of events to fulfil a purpose, something brilliant and dazzling in the execution, a kind of luring and forcing Fortune to obey one, as with that type of all heroes, Julius Cæsar? This is nearer the truth, but does not account for those heroes who were not successful. Thus Leonidas the heroic was overpowered by superior strategy. Nor does it account for men like Ludendorff or Rockefeller, possessed of resource, success, and brilliance, but very far from being heroes.

The truth seems to be that heroism is not something that can be defined from the quality of the hero's character alone. The circumstances make the hero. We do not advance Tolstoy's conception of the hero, a man of petty stature borne on the tide of fortune. There must be something in the man. But there must also be something in events. The conception of the hero as the man dominating and moulding circumstances to his will is as false as that of him simply lifted to achievement as on a wave of the sea. Or rather both are partial aspects of the same truth, that of the freedom of man's will.

Man's will is free so far as it is consciously self-determined. His will at any moment is determined by the causal influences of his environment and his immediately preceding mental state, including in his mental state all those physiological factors that combine in the conscious and unconscious innervation patterns. A man is born with certain innate responses determined by his heredity, in a certain environment determined by the past. As he lives his life, innate responses and environment interact to form his consciousness, which is thus the result of a mutual tension between environment and instinct, begetting a continual development of the mind. Since all action involves an equal and opposite reaction, he in turn changes the environment during each transaction which changes him. His environment of course includes other human beings.

A hero is a man whose life is such that, his instinctive equipment being what it is, and his environment being what it is, the effect he has on his environment is much greater than the effect it has on him. We may, therefore, say that he is a man who dominates and moulds his environment.

But, just as a man can only carve a chicken properly if he knows where the joints are, and follows them, so a hero dominates events only because he conforms closely with the law that produces them. The man masterfully carving a chicken therefore corresponds also to the Tolstoyan conception of the hero as a man who is really a slave to circumstances. There is only one way of carving a chicken perfectly, and therefore the man who completely dominates the chicken by carving it perfectly is also completely dominated by it in that he has to follow its anatomy slavishly. But all the same it ends by being carved up. Even this makes the situation seem too simple. For there is also a cause in the dialectic of man's life why he wants to carve the chicken, why the hero wants to shake worlds.

Here we come to another characteristic of heroism, that the hero, even as he alters the world, seems unaware of what he is doing. Cæsar never consciously willed the Imperiate, nor Alexander the birth of Hellenistic culture. And yet they willed something, and all their actions seemed directed to the ends they brought about.

The hero seems to act with a kind of blind intuition ; and it is therefore particularly strange that the hero is master equally of matter and men, a thing foreign to the abilities of most great men. In this the hero fades on the one hand into the prophet or religious teacher, who can control men's souls but cannot control events, and on the other hand into the scientist, who can teach men how to control events if they wish, but cannot teach them what to wish. The hero understands geography, war, politics, and cities, and new techniques are instrumental to him, but men are instrumental to him too. And with it all he hardly knows why it is so ; he could not give a causal explanation of what is to come about in the future in conformity with his present action, but it seems as if he knows in his heart what to do. A goddess, like Cæsar's divine patron and ancestor, Venus, seems to watch over his relations with men and events.

From whence does this gift spring ? What is its meaning ? Often the last thing the hero wishes to do is what he actually does. Like Cæsar he may be at heart a mere adventurer, and yet this knack of heroism ensures that in making his career he creates a civilisation, and irradiates his name with an almost divine lustre, while strenuous altruists are forgotten, or if remembered are remembered like the Inquisitors with execration. This quality of heroism is then independent of their motives, and yet it is a value, and must adhere to something.

It adheres to the social significance of their acts. Their desires arise from the movement of social relations, and the same movement is the force they wield, the magical power which seems to make the stars in their courses fight for them.

All crises, all wars, all perils or triumphs of States, all changes of social systems in which the hero manifests himself, represent the cracking of the carapace of social consciousness and all its organised formulations beneath the internal pressure of changed social being. If social being were never to change, social consciousness, which bodies forth underlying social reality in terms of static symbols (words, thoughts, concepts, images, churches, laws), would always be adequate, and society would revolve like a gyroscope, stable and stationary. But in fact reality is never the same, for to say that it is the same means that time is at an end. Time is simply an unlikeness in events of a particular inclusive character, such that A is included by B, B by C, and so on. Becoming is intrinsic in reality which is therefore always cracking its skin, not gradually but like a snake, in seasons. The pressure rises until in a crisis the whole skin is cast. The superstructure of society is regrown.

At such times there is a tumult of action and thought, but since action precedes thought, the right thing must be done before the right thought can come into being. Social consciousness is not a mirror-image of social being. If it were, it would be useless, a mere fantasy. It is material, possessed of mass and inertia, composed of real things—philosophies, language habits, churches, judiciaries, police. If social consciousness were but a mirror-image, it could change like an image without the expenditure of energy when the object which it mirrored changed. But it is more than that. It is a functional superstructure which interacts with the foundations, each altering the other. There is a coming-and-going between them. So, life, arising from dead matter, turns back on it and changes it. The process is evident in the simplest use of language. The word is social, representing existing conscious formulations. But to wish to speak, we wish to say something new, arising from our life experience, from our being. And, therefore, we use the Word, with a metaphor or in a sentence, in such a way that it has a slightly fresh significance nearer to our own new experience. This process on a vast scale produces revolutions, when men dissatisfied with the inherited social formulations of reality—governments, institutions and laws—wish to remake them nearer to their new and as yet unformulated experience. And because such institutions, unlike words, possess inertia, because the men with new experience represent one class, and the men without it clinging to the old formulations represent another class, the process is violent and energetic.

Man himself is composed like society of current active being and inherited conscious formulations. He is somatic and psychic, instinctive and conscious, and these opposites interpenetrate. He is formed, half rigid, in the shape of the culture he was born in, half fluid and new and insurgent, sucking reality through his instinctive roots. Thus he feels, right in the heart of him, this tension between being and thinking, between new being and old thought, a tension which will give rise by synthesis to new thought. He feels as if the deepest instinctive part of him and the most valuable is being dragged away from his consciousness by events. The incomplete future is dragging at him, but because instinctive components of the psyche are the oldest, he often feels this to be the past dragging at him. That is why so often we come upon the paradox that the hero appeals to the past, and urges men to bring it into being again, and in doing so, produces the future. The return to the classics dominated the bourgeois Renaissance. Rome influenced Napoleon and the Revolution. The return to the natural uncorrupted man was the ideal of eighteenth-century revolutionaries. Yet it is the new whose tension men feel in their minds and hearts at such times. The new, implicit and informous, waits at the portals of man's consciousness. But it is invisible. It is as yet only a force, a tension, adequate to make of the things which generate that tension a new and synthesised reality, but at this stage no clearer than a force, a bodiless power. When he hears this signal, imperious in its call to action, the hero will as likely as not give it a formulation from the obscure past, since he cannot clothe it in the unknown qualities of the future. Coming as it does, not from the established habits of society and of his mind but from a pressure in the depths of both, this call to action seems to arise from the depths of man's soul. Therefore, he interprets it either as a personal devouring ambition (as indeed, in a sense it is) or as a call from God (as in another sense it is, for God always appears as a symbol of unconscious social relations). The mystic and the artist feel the same force, but they do not feel it as the hero does. To him it is a call to bring actively into the world this unknown thing, by shattering the material embodiments that oppose it or by creating new forms to receive it. He may think it is the past he is born to save or re-establish on earth and only when it is done is it seen that the future has come into being. The reformer 'returning' to primitive Christianity brings bourgeois Protestantism into being; and the adventurer raising himself by destroying senatorial power creates the Roman Imperiate.

Concerned chiefly with action, the hero reasons crudely, for action not reason is his task. His ideals are crude; his aims perhaps personal, selfish, and mean. But we are not concerned with these. Watch his deeds. These express the force that is guiding him, and by these he conquers. Thus for all his irrationality he overcomes the more intellectual and enlightened spirits of his age. Wise and far-seeing men, perhaps, but they speak only the language of the present; and are caught in the conscious formulations of their past. He speaks no known language, only a preposterous mixture of childhood memories and half-baked notions. But he acts a philosophy wiser than that professed by his academic opponents. Cicero goes down before Cæsar for Cæsar speaks the language of to-morrow, and Alexander with the intelligence and manners of a public school cad has yet advanced to the Hellenistic empire while Aristotle is wasting his pupils' time in investigating the constitutions of 158 obsolete city states. Although the hero's language is mixed and self-contradictory, his hearers are in no doubt as to what he refers. They too have heard that call to action from the heart of reality and have felt the growing tension in their hearts. For its sake they are prepared to abandon consciousness; for it is the consciousness of past obsolete experience. Reason—all the arguments based correctly on premises that have since changed—is powerless to silence this voice.

They believe they are turning from consciousness and reason to the voice of the heart and of the instincts. They believe they are abandoning the wretched present for the golden past. But in fact, as history always shows, they are abandoning present consciousness only to synthesise it in a wider consciousness and it is not to the golden past they turn, but the golden future. Hero and followers, leader and revolutionaries speak the same almost intuitive language, for they learn it from the same source. The hero may talk wildly or be dumb, may be ridiculous and contradictory, yet his audience knows to what he refers and how it cannot be expressed in words, only in action. From this arises the hero's masterful power over men. This power seems unconscious. Precisely because it is generated in reaching out, through action, to the consciousness of the new reality, it seems most true when least in the region of conscious formulation. The hero seems most successful when he follows blindly what he calls Luck or Inspiration or Divine Guidance, and what we as mystically call Intuition. That typical hero Cromwell explained this in his revealing comment to the French envoy Bellièvre:

'No one rises so high as he who knows not whither he is going.'

Every hero from Alexander to Napoleon might take this as his motto.

Yet the very source of this power outside the sphere of contemporary consciousness has its dangers. For the power, just because it does not consciously know its goal, may be wasted in a useless explosion. Because all men feel at such times, in the same vague and unformulated way the tension in society pressing for an outlet, they may be the prey of any charlatan who speaks a mystical language calling for change. The force will be tapped that could move mountains, but here the charlatan is as blind as they. For this is the difference between the charlatan and the hero. The charlatan has power over men but not over matter. He does not know the joints of the chicken of circumstance. He leads men back into abandoned ways and forgotten heresies.

For at such a time, because of the force that is being generated, there must be motion. The sum of things is tottering and man must go either backwards or forwards. Just as the neurotic goes back to a childhood solution, faced with impossible adult problems, so civilisation in times of stress such as we have pictured may move towards a previous solution, to some golden age of autocracy or feudalism which once was fertile. But the past can never be again. Just because the present has intervened, nothing can ever be as it once was. The fabric of society has become too changed and subtle to take up the old shape. Like the neurosis, social regression is no solution.

The charlatan appears at the same time as the hero, superficially like him, created by the same forces, and yet playing an opposite rôle. He is a Sulla, a Kerensky, a Hitler or a Mussolini. Hitler and Mussolini draw their power from the same source as Lenin drew his, from the tension between capitalist social relations and the growth in productive forces. And by the usual irony of revolutions, these charlatans appear at first as angels of construction and conservation and the hero seems the destructive element. Only later is it seen that their rôle is opposite, that the charlatans by wasting men's energy in vain regression are disintegrating all social relations, and that the hero by the very movement that sweeps the old forms off the stage brings into being the new.

Heroes are known not only by their power over men, which charlatans share, but over events, over external reality, over matter. Their intuition of the new social reality extends beyond a knowledge of the tension between the two and teaches them, not fully and clearly but enough for action, the path to be followed to give this tension a creative issue. Thus they move prophetically towards the future and act according to history, history in an unfair manner therefore seeming to play into their hands while all that the charlatans tried to build is swept away by time. The hero may die before he sees himself justified, but we say rightly, that his teaching lives on. He fought for things that survive him, and what can survive the present but the future ? This was the world to which he belonged, and we who live in it accord him the greeting of a fellow-citizen and all the admiration felt by a stay-at-home for a colonist.

Heroes are born with the aptitude perhaps, but are made by circumstances. And there is something peculiarly instructive as to the nature of heroes in the example of the bourgeois, Lawrence, dowered with all the hero's legendary gifts, called to action and yet through circumstances unable to answer the call. A man of unusual force of personality, intense ambition, and rare intellectual ability, Lawrence showed from his early years a strange restlessness. This restlessness of the hero is not unusual. It is as if from the beginning he feels in his heart the tension of the new social relations, but it is at first an appetite without an object. With Lawrence as with other heroes the splendid past was to engross that appetite and not merely in the form of his technical interest in archæology, but also as an attraction to the something large and vivid that there was in the ancient world, submerged in the tawdriness of modern conditions, so that he was driven to wander through the spacious deserts of the primitive East.

The nostalgia which afflicted him was plain enough. It was for ampler social relations, purged of the pettiness and commercialisation of capitalism. Every stage in his life derives its explanation only from this ruling need. As a kind of scholar gipsy he rubbed shoulders in his youth with all classes and conditions of the East. He found his nostalgia satisfied to the greatest degree by the free and open manners of the Bedouin. Their freedom and the value they attached to character and leadership fascinated him, revolted as he was by a world in which value attached only to cash. His hatred of the bourgeois present and the call of the future were symbolised to him by a golden age, the spacious and simple vividness of the Odyssey. This noble life was not entirely dead, he found. In Arabia Deserta, a corner of the world as yet free from capitalist exploitation, this classic simplicity of society still lived on. True, he found that this desert culture could never fully sate the hunger that sent him on his travels. But he did not ask himself if after all the desires were what they clothed themselves in, whether it was in fact the past he hungered for. He explained it differently : they were Arabs and he was European ; they were simple and he was over-educated and sophisticated.

Then came the War, and with it the opportunity to give liberty to these people so precious to him because he saw in them all that he yearned for and could not find. And here Lawrence failed of the hero's grip on changing reality. Liberty—the word to him came simply with all the bourgeois conscious formulations he had absorbed at Oxford, and with it mingled the freedom he had experienced in the tents of the Bedouins, and the word seemed only an enlargement of the same gifts. He did not ask whether these liberties were the same, and if different, what bourgeois liberty really meant. Liberty was the gift he would give them. That was enough. He could act on that clear and classic issue.

So for a time he mastered men and events. He mastered men, because both he and the Arabs were in love with social relations free from the money taint, open, frank, and equal. Theirs was the openness of the past, and what appealed to him was a frankness of the future ; but he did not know this, nor could he, there in Arabia Deserta. He, too, humbly twisted his ideals to theirs. His openness drew nothing from the future, but was crammed into an Arab dress, bloody, barbarous, without faith, and merciful only to those whose bread and salt it has shared. He cramped it into a liberty shared by a few men, savage and ignorant, disdainful of the rest of humanity. Here was something not without good because it was free and human ; but because of its limitations it was unworthy of a bourgeois hero nourished on Plato and Xenophon. It was still more unworthy of a hero who had felt in his heart the emptiness of bourgeoisdom and the call of a new world. He had desired to be just and friendly and brave and to hate pomp and ceremony and wealth, and to love the essence of a man simply as it realised itself in action. These values, lost to the bourgeois world, and only partially and primitively realised among the Bedouins, are the core of communist honour. But he crushed them into the mould of a desert Arab—he who had tasted all the philosophy and art of bourgeois Europe. He slew and plundered and was ruthless and contracted his aspirations to the narrow hopes of an Arab leader. Afterwards all this blood or wasted effort and vain tension were to reproach him like a murdered opportunity.

Why was he able to show this gift of the hero, to master in this limited sphere as well as men the march of events ? Because he knew intuitively how stiff and indurated and obsolete capitalist social relations had become. The Conquistadors in the springtime of the bourgeoisie when these developing social relations seemed sweet and golden could conquer without help a whole New World. One handful of them could master a dead civilisation. But now the bourgeois had grown stiff-jointed. In Arabia, as on the battle-fields of Flanders, the bourgeois fighting-machine had become as obsolete as a mammoth. A feudal society could baffle it. Lawrence was the first to make this discovery, and with his intuitive knowledge he struck at the weak points of the bourgeois fighting-machine, at its clumsy technical organisation, its inefficiency, its dependence on supplies. Moreover, simply because he loathed the values of bourgeois society, he could sway the minds of desert Arabs. Even, most difficult task of all, he could bribe without offence a patriarchal people to whom, unlike a bourgeois class, money is not everything, the sole bond of society.

So Lawrence freed Arabia. But what had he freed it for ? If one frees a society whose social organisation belongs to the past, but has been preserved by a decadent autocracy, what can it do but advance to the present ? If one gives a country liberty as the bourgeois understands it, liberty to be a self-governnig 'independent' bourgeois state, what can come into being there but bourgeois social relations ?

So the Arabs Lawrence freed met two fates, apparently dissimilar but in essence the same. Some became part of the French Empire. Others were permitted to set up under British tutelage but with a king of their own blood, a complete bourgeois state, Iraq, with government, police, oil concessions, and all the other bourgeois paraphernalia.

Lawrence felt that he and the British Government had betrayed some of the Arabs. But he never fully realised how completely he had betrayed them all. He had brought into Arabia the very evil he had fled. Soon his desert Arabs would have money, businesses, investments, loud-speakers, and regular employment. But he could not realise this consciously, for he had never been fully conscious that it was bourgeois social relations he was fleeing, and he was not aware of the omnipotent destructive power of the present over the past. He was in fact like a man who, fleeing blindly from a deadly disease to a healthy land, himself afflicts it with the plague. Had he fully realised all this, he could also have comforted himself with the reflection that it was inevitable, that the past must bow to the present unless, indeed, as in Russia, it can invoke a stronger ally, and because the future is already ripe for delivery in the womb of the present, bring the future into being. Such work demands not only heroes, but that the future is ready to appear, is already fully implicit. And it is not so in the wilds of Arabia.

Thus Lawrence could not realise clearly what had happened, but this he could realise, that Syria and Iraq were no answer to the nostalgia of his life and no great issue to his ruthless and extravagant expense of spirit.

In those bitter after-days Lawrence still heard that imperious call and tasted all the decay of dying bourgeois culture. He saw this decay in all State ceremony, in all the politenesses of society in the glare of 'publicity'. On every manifestation of bourgeois culture he saw the same dreadful slime. Only in the ranks of the Army he found a stunted version of his ideal, barren of fulfilment but at least free from dishonour. In the Army, at least, though men have taken the King's shilling, it is not the search for profit that holds the fabric together, but it is based on a simple social imperative and wields a force that never reckons its dividends. Like a kind of Arabian desert in the heart of the vulgar luxury of bourgeoisdom, the bare tents of the Army shield a simple comradeship, a social existence free from competition or hate. It is both survival and anticipation, for on the one hand it conserves old feudal relations, as they were before bourgeoisdom burst them, and on the other hand it prophesies like a rudimentary symbol the community of to-morrow united by ties of common effort and not of cash. This man desperately sick of bourgeois relations found in the Services something not found elsewhere, a comradeship of work as well as play, a sterile and yet comforting reminder of finer things. In peace the unproductive labour of a Fighting Service irks it, and fills the members in spite of their comradeship with a constant nagging sense of impotence. But when war comes and the issues of society are put into its hands by a bourgeoisie which in emergency is prepared to abandon the arbitrament of cash and law for the arbitrament of blood and violence to protect or extend its own—then an Army realises itself. In spite of all war's horror and dangers, a kind of wild elation and well-being fills it, and millions of men who fought in the war can testify to the collective delirium that lifted them out of the greyness of bourgeois existence.

Even this peace-time impotence was better to Lawrence than the bourgeois relations which his soul revolted at. So he entered a Fighting Service. Not as an officer. It was bourgeoisdom he detested, and it would have been impossible for him to enter that class which preserved even in the Army the characteristics he loathed. He entered the ranks. He showed by this gesture his intuitive knowledge that the nostalgia of his life was for the future, the world of the proletariat. But still the conscious forms of his education prevented him from understanding himself.

He embraced, not only the proletariat, but the machine. In those bitter later years, machines had a fascination for him. The aeroplane, the motor-cycle and the motor-boat seemed to him entities somehow possessed of a strange power for man. He said and wrote that to participate in the conquest of the air was at least a work not altogether vain, yet why he could not say. With the machine was the future; and yet it was not in the machine as a profit-maker that he was interested.

He was right. In the machine lay the significance he sought. But not in the machine as mere machine, but in the machine consciously controlled by man, by whose use he could regain the freedom and equality of primitive relations without losing the rich consciousness of the ages of European culture. The instrument was in Lawrence's hands, as it is in bourgeois hands, but like them he did not know how to use it. Like the bourgeoisie he became intoxicated with the giddy sense of power of this machine, careering to disaster on it, supposing that he controlled it because it went faster and faster. They found him one day unconscious beside his huge motor-cycle, which he had not learned to control. A few days later Lawrence was dead.

What halted Lawrence on the nearside of achievement so that instead of becoming the communist hero, which his gifts and his hatred for the evils of capitalism fitted him for, he became a bourgeois hero who miscarried? Lawrence's tragedy was partly due to his education. He was too intellectual. The hero should have plenty of native intelligence, but to be intellectual means that one's psychic potentialities have been fully developed into the current forms. Lawrence was a man of high consciousness, but it was the consciousness of a culture now doomed. All the outworn symbols of the long noonday of bourgeois culture stiffened his prodigious memory, and made of his genius an elaborate osseous structure too tenacious for the instinctive movement of his soul. That is why thought, devised only to aid action, yet often seems to hamper action. Lawrence himself believed that his was the tragedy of the man of action who is also a thinker. This was to make his tragedy too simple. The deadlock was more profound and significant.

Other heroes have been educated and have overcome it in struggling for the past; they have achieved the future. Why could not he? A new factor entered into Lawrence's tragedy which can best be understood by considering Lenin. Lenin is a hero of a stamp so different from the heroes of the past that one is tempted at first to revise one's definition of the hero. The hero of past history was impelled by social forces he did not understand, whose power he symbolised in vague aspirations. Often he thought it was the past he was trying to create, or like a Joan of Arc he was following simply 'Divine Guidance', or 'Voices'. Such heroes create the future darkly, unaware of what they do or why they do it.

Lenin had no doubt as to his task. The future he had to call into being was Communist society and he knew how it was contained within and could be released from bourgeois social relations. He did not merely know this intuitively but all is clearly set down in his speeches and writings. He did not know the distinctive qualities of the future, for no one can know these, but he knew its general shape and the most important causal laws shaping social relations just as the scientist without knowing the qualities of the future knows certain causal laws that enable him to predict the tides and if necessary take advantage of them. This is the essence of prediction: a certain continuity of like persists in the process of reality and is the substrate of the continual development of the unlike which is Becoming. Like and unlike are not mutually exclusive entities, but one becomes another, and the change of one is the change of another. Quality just because it is unlike emerges suddenly, dialectically, as a new mutation. Quantity changes only gradually: it remains within the ambit of known relations. It is always the like with which science is concerned—the electron, time, space, radiation, and the conservation laws connecting them. Because it restricts its attention to known relations science can predict the knowable element in the future. To this degree the scientist of sociology can know the future. This Lenin did. But the heroes of old were necessarily ignorant even of the quantitative basis of the future. Lenin, although a man of action, was thus devoid of the mysticism, the 'lucky' character of the hero, and took on much of the cognitive character of the scientist.

Yet was not this development essential in a man who was to bring to birth a society whose essence, distinguishing it from all earlier social relations, is that in it human beings are cognitively conscious of social relations, and understand not merely the environment of society like bourgeois culture, but society itself? Only the self-conscious hero could lead man towards the self-conscious society. If the characteristic of communism was to be that it would replace religion, mysticism, 'race', and all the symbolical formulations in which men have clothed their dark intuitions of the true nature of social relations, the banner-bearers of communism must be equally freed of myth and illusion. Such men must not see society as the active theatre of gods, demons, or vague statuesque personifications of Liberty,

Fraternity and the Natural Man, but as it is in its causality. Lenin was able to do this, for Marx had already exposed the causal laws of society. Lenin, then, begins the new race of heroes or leaders just as Hitler and Mussolini stand at the end of the long illustrious line of anti-heroes or charlatans. It is not possible now for the hero, guided by an instinctive feeling, to do the right thing against his own intellectual limitations. Such heroes will like Lawrence only be strangled by their own consciousnesses. The very demand of communism, that man be conscious not merely of what he wills but of what determines that will, requires an equal consciousness of a communist leader.

It was Lawrence's tragedy that he was baffled not merely by his intellectualism, but by the very nature of the new world whose cry for deliverance he had heard in his dreams. Other heroes, despite the distorting bias of yesterday's consciousness, have managed to find the right path, pulled along it by the overwhelming force of the day's experience. But no more such 'instinctive' heroes are to be born. Before Lawrence could be a hero, it was not enough to disregard his consciousness, he had first to shatter it and build it anew on a wider and firmer basis. And how could he find that new consciousness in the groves of Oxford, or in the stark Arabian waste, still virginal to market and machine?

Thus the task of the heroes of to-morrow is more strenuous and yet more satisfying than that of the strong ones who lived before Lenin. They must first know what it is they help to bring to birth, but knowing it they will know also that they *can* bring it to birth, that they are dependent, not on luck, on divine inspiration, or on an ancestral Aphrodite, but that they are part of the causality which is the self-determination of the Universe. This is the end of the hero who lives a myth and of the fairy-tales he tells his followers. The childhood of the human race, with all its appealing simplicity and pretty make-believe, is past, and its heroes too must be adult.

In China, too, a race of simple and peasant people, of millions captive to poverty and insolence, have been stirred to action by the name of liberty. It is not a story of one hero, but of an army of heroes, performing exploits believed impossible, not aided by bourgeois gold, but repelling again and again attacks financed by bourgeois gold, armed by bourgeois powers, directed by bourgeois experts. This national rising, led by the Red Army of China, and growing constantly in fire and influence, is also inspired by the name of liberty, but it is not bourgeois liberty. Bourgeois liberty, in the shape of Japanese Imperialism, British banking, and American trade, unites with the bourgeois Kuomintang Government to crush it. The Red Army is a Communist Army, and wherever it moves it establishes village soviets. Its leaders and its rank and file have read the words of Marx, Lenin and Stalin. While oil finance tightens its clutches on Iraq, creation of Lawrence, the liberator, the bourgeois hero, Chinese nationalism, baffled and outraged for so long, finds its last ardent victorious issue in Communism.

III

D. H. LAWRENCE

A STUDY OF THE BOURGEOIS ARTIST

WHAT is the function of the artist? Any artist such as Lawrence, who aims to be 'more than' an artist, necessarily raises this question. It is supposed to be the teaching of Marxism that art for art's sake is an illusion and that art must be propaganda. This is, however, making the usual bourgeois simplification of a complex matter.

Art is a social function. This is not a Marxist demand, but arises from the very way in which art forms are defined. Only those things are recognised as art forms which have a conscious social function. The phantasies of a dreamer are not art. They only become art when they are given music, forms or words, when they are clothed in socially recognised symbols, and of course in the process there is a modification. The phantasies are modified by the social dress; the language as a whole acquires new associations and context. No chance sounds constitute music, but sounds selected from a socially recognised scale and played on socially developed instruments.

It is not for Marxism therefore to demand that art

play a social function or to attack the conception of 'art for art's sake', for art only *is* art, and recognisable as such, in so far as it plays a social function. What is of importance to art, Marxism and society is the question: *What social function is art playing?* This in turn depends on the type of society in which it is secreted.

In bourgeois society social relations are denied in the form of relations between men, and take the form of a relation between man and a thing, a property relation, which, because it is a dominating relation, is believed to make man free. But this is an illusion. The property relation is only a disguise for relations which now become unconscious and therefore anarchic but are still between man and man and in particular between exploiter and exploited.

The artist in bourgeois culture is asked to do the same thing. He is asked to regard the art work as a finished commodity and the process of art as a relation between himself and the work, which then disappears into the market. There is a further relation between the art work and the buyer, but with this he can hardly be immediately concerned. The whole pressure of bourgeois society is to make him regard the art work as hypostatised and his relation to it as primarily that of a producer for the market.

This will have two results.

(i) The mere fact that he has to earn his living by the sale of the concrete hypostatised entity as a property right—copyright, picture, statue—may drive him to estimate his work as an artist by the market chances which produce a high total return for these property rights. This leads to the commercialisation or vulgarisation of art.

(ii) But art is not in any case a relation to a thing, it is a relation between men, between artist and audience, and the art work is only like a machine which they must both grasp as part of the process. The commercialisation of art may revolt the sincere artist, but the tragedy is that he revolts against it still within the limitations of bourgeois culture. He attempts to forget the market completely and concentrate on his relation to the art work, which now becomes still further hypostatised as an entity-in-itself. Because the art work is now completely an end-in-itself, and even the market is forgotten, the art process becomes an extremely individualistic relation. The social values inherent in the art form, such as syntax, tradition, rules, technique, form, accepted tonal scale, now seem to have little value, for the art work more and more exists for the individual alone. The art work is necessarily always the product of a tension between old conscious social formulations—the art 'form'—and new individual experience made conscious—the art 'content' or the artist's 'message'. This is the synthesis, the specifically hard task of creation. But the hypostatisation of the art work as the goal makes old conscious social formulations less and less important, and individual experience more and more dominating. As a result art becomes more and more formless, personal, and individualistic, culminating in Dadaism, surréalism and ' Steining '.

Thus bourgeois art disintegrates under the tension of two forces, both arising from the same feature of bourgeois culture. On the one hand there is production for the market—vulgarisation, commercialisation. On the other there is hypostatisation of the art work as the goal of the art process, and the relation between art work and individual as paramount. This necessarily leads to a dissolution of those social values which make the art in question a social relation, and therefore ultimately results in the art work's ceasing to be an art work and becoming a mere private phantasy.

All bourgeois art during the last two centuries shows the steady development of this bifurcation. As long as the social values inherent in an art form are not disintegrated—e.g. up to say 1910—the artist who hypostatises the art form and despises the market can produce good art. After that, it becomes steadily more difficult. Needless to say, the complete acceptance of the market, being a refusal to regard any part of the art process as a social process, is even more incompetent to produce great art. Anything which helps the artist to escape from the bourgeois trap and become conscious of social relations inherent in art, will help to delay the rot. For this reason the novel is the last surviving literary art form in bourgeois culture, for in it, for reasons explained elsewhere, the social relations inherent in the art process are overt. Dorothy Richardson, James Joyce, and Proust, all in different ways are the last blossoms of the bourgeois novel, for with them the novel begins to disappear as an objective study of social relations and becomes a study of the subject's experience in society. It is then only a step for the thing experienced to disappear and, as in Gertrude Stein, for complete 'me-ness' to reign.

It is inevitable that at this stage the conception of the artist as a pure 'artist' must cease to exist. For commercialised art has become intolerably base and negated itself. And equally art for art's sake (that is, the ignoring of the market and concentration on the perfect art work as a goal in itself) has negated itself, for the art form has ceased to exist, and what was art has become private phantasy. It is for this reason that sincere artists, such as Lawrence, Gide, Romain Rolland, Romains and so on, cannot be content with the beautiful art work, but seem to desert the practice of art for social theory and become novelists of ideas, literary prophets and propaganda novelists. They represent the efforts of bourgeois art, exploded into individualistic phantasy and commercialised muck, to become once more a social process and so be reborn. Whether such art is or can be great art is beside the point, since it is inevitably the pre-requisite for art becoming art again, just as it is beside the point whether the transition from bourgeoisdom to communism is itself smooth or happy or beautiful or free, since it is the inevitable step if bourgeois anarchy and misery is to be healed and society to become happy and free.

But what is art as a social process? What is art, not

as a mere art work or a means of earning a living, but in itself, the part it plays in society ? I have dealt fully with this point elsewhere, and need only briefly recapitulate now.

The personal phantasy or day-dream is not art, however beautiful. Nor is the beautiful sunset. Both are only the raw material of art. It is the property of art that it makes mimic pictures of reality which we accept as illusory. We do not suppose the events of a novel really happen, that a landscape shown on a painting can be walked upon—yet it has a measure of reality.

The mimic representation, by the technique appropriate to the art in question, causes the social representation to sweat out of its pores an affective emanation. The emanation is *in* us, *in* our affective reaction with the elements of the representation. Given in the representation are not only the affects, but, simultaneously, their organisation in an affective *attitude* towards the piece of reality symbolised in the mimicry. This affective attitude is bitten in by a general heightening of consciousness and increase in self-value, due to the non-motor nature of the innervations aroused, which seems therefore all to pass into an affective irradiation of consciousness. This affective attitude is not permanent, as is the intellectual attitude towards reality aroused by a cogent scientific argument, but still—because of the mnemic characteristics of an organism—it remains as an *experience* and must, therefore, in proportion to the amount of conscious poignancy accompanying the experience and the nature of the experience, modify the subject's general attitude towards life itself. This modification tends to make life more interesting to the organism, hence the survival value of art. But viewed from society's standpoint, art is the fashioning of the affective consciousness of its members, the conditioning of their instincts.

Language, simply because it is the most general instrument for communicating views of reality, whether affective and cognitive, has a particularly fluid range of representations of reality. Hence the suppleness and scope of literary art ; the novel, the drama, the poem, the short story, and the essay. It can draw upon all the symbolic pictures of reality made by scientific, historical and discursive intellectual processes. Art can only achieve its purpose if the pictures themselves are made simultaneously to produce affect and organisation. Then, even as the artist holds up to us the piece of reality, it seems already glowing with affective colouring.

Reality constitutes for us our environment ; and our environment, which is chiefly social, alters continuously—sometimes barely perceptibly, sometimes at dizzy speeds. The socially accepted pictures we make in words of reality cannot change as if they were reflections in a mirror. An object is reflected in a mirror. If the object moves the reflection moves. But in language reality is symbolised in unchanging words, which give a false stability and permanence to the object they represent. Thus they instantaneously photograph reality rather than reflect it. This frigid character of language is regrettable but it has its utilitarian purposes. It is probably the only way in which man, with his linear consciousness, can get a grip of fluid reality. Language, as it develops, shows more and more of this false permanence, till we arrive at the Platonic Ideas, Eternal and Perfect Words. Their eternity and perfection is simply the permanence of print and paper. If you coin a word or write a symbol to describe an entity or event, the word will remain 'eternally' unchanged even while the entity has changed and the event is no longer present. This permanence is part of the inescapable nature of symbolism, which is expressed in the rules of logic. It is one of the strange freaks of the human mind that it has supposed that reality must obey the rules of logic, whereas the correct view is that symbolism by its very nature has certain rules, expressed in the laws of logic, and these are nothing to do with the process of reality, but represent the nature of the symbolic process itself.

The artist experiences this discrepancy between language and reality as follows : he has had an intense experience of a rose and wishes to communicate his experience to his fellows in words. He wishes to say, 'I saw a rose'. But 'rose' has a definite social meaning, or group of meanings, and we are to suppose that he has had an experience with the rose which does not correspond to any of society's previous experiences of roses, embodied in the word and its history. His experience of the rose is therefore the negation of the word 'rose', it is 'not-rose'—all that in his experience which is not expressed in the current social meaning of the word 'rose'. He therefore says—'I saw a rose like'—and there follows a metaphor, or there is an adjective—'a heavenly rose', or a euphemism—'I saw a flowery blush', and in each case there is a synthesis, for his new experience has become socially fused into society's old experiences and both have been changed in the process. His own experience has taken colour from all past meanings of the word 'rose', for these will be present in men's minds when they read his poem, and the word 'rose' will have taken colour from his individual experience, for his poem will in future be in men's minds when they encounter the word 'rose'.

But why was the poet's experience different from society's tradition? Because that cross-section of his environment which we call his individual life-experience was different. But if we take all society's art as a whole, i.e. the sum of individual cross-sections, we get on the one hand the whole experience of the environment averaged out, and also the average man, or average genotype. Now the constant genesis of new art must mean that the environment is changing, so that man's individual experiences are changing, and he is constantly finding inherited social conscious formulations inadequate and requiring resynthesis. Thus if art forms remain unchanged and traditional, as in Chinese civilisation, it is evident that the environment—social relations—are static. If they decay the environment is on the down-grade, as with current bourgeois culture. If they improve, the reverse is the case. But the artist's value is not in *self*-expression. If so, why should he struggle to achieve the synthesis in which old social formulations are fused with his individual experience? Why not disregard social formalities and express himself direct as one does by shouting, leaping, and cries? Because, to begin with, it is the old bourgeois illusion to suppose there is such a thing as pure individual expression. It is not even that the artist nobly forces his self-expression into a social mould for the benefit of society. Both attitudes are simply expressions of the old bourgeois fallacy that man is free in freely giving vent to his instincts. In fact the artist does not express himself in art forms, he finds himself therein. He does not adulterate his free self-expression to make it socially current, he finds free self-expression only in the social relations embodied in art. The value of art to the artist then is this, that it makes him free. It appears to him of value as a self-expression, but in fact is is not the expression of a self but the discovery of a self. It is the creation of a self. In synthesising experience with society's, in pressing his inner self into the mould of social relations, he not only creates a new mould, a socially valuable product, but he also moulds and creates his own self. The mute inglorious Milton is a fallacy. Miltons are made not born.

The value of art to society is that by it an emotional adaptation is possible. Man's instincts are pressed in art against the altered mould of reality, and by a specific organisation of the emotions thus generated, there is a new attitude, an *adaptation*.

All art is produced by this tension between changing social relations and outmoded consciousness. The very reason why new art is created, why the old art does not satisfy either artist or appreciator, is because it seems somehow out of gear with the present. Old art always has meaning for us, because the instincts, the source of the affects, do not change, because a new system of social relations does not exclude but includes the old, and because new art too includes the traditions of the art that has gone before. But it is not enough. We must have new art.

And new art results from tension. This tension takes two forms. (i) One is productive—the evolutionary form. The tension between productive relations and productive forces secures the advance of society as a whole, simply by producing in an even more pronounced form the contradiction which was the source of the dynamism. Thus bourgeois culture by continually dissolving the relations between men for relations to a thing, and thus hypostatising the market, procured the growth of industrial capitalism. And, in the sphere of art it produced the increasing individualism which, seen at its best in Shakespeare, was a positive value, but pushed to its limit finally spelt the complete breakdown of art in surréalism, Dadaism and Steinism.

(ii) The tension now becomes revolutionary. For productive relations are a brake on productive forces and the tension between them, instead of altering productive relations in the direction of giving better outlet to productive forces, has the opposite effect. It drives productive relations on still further into negation, increases the tension, and prepares the explosion which will shatter the old productive relations and enable them to be rebuilt anew—not arbitrarily, but according to a pattern which will itself be given by the circumstances of the tension. Thus in art the tension between individualism and the increasing complexity and catastrophes of the artist's environment, between the free following of dream and the rude blows of anarchic reality, wakes the artist from his dream and forces him in spite of himself to look at the world, not merely as an artist, but also as a man, as a citizen, as a sociologist. It forces him to be interested in things not strictly germane to art ;—politics, economics, science, and philosophy, just as it did during the early bourgeois Renaissance, producing ' all-round men ' like Leonardo da Vinci. Whether this is good for art or not is beside the point. Bourgeois art like bourgeois culture is moribund and this process is an inevitable concomitant of the stage proceeding art's rebirth. And because of this intervening period, the new art when it emerges will be art more conscious of itself as part of the whole social process, will be *communist* art. This explains why all modern artists of any significance such as Lawrence, Gide, Aragon, dos Passos, Eliot and so on, cannot be content to be ' pure ' artists, but must also be prophets, thinkers, philosophers, and politicians, men interested in life and social reality as a whole. They are conscious of having a message. This is the inevitable effect on art of a revolutionary period, and it is not possible to escape from it into 'pure' art, into the ivory tower, for now there is no pure art ; that phase is either over or not yet begun.

But at a revolution two paths are possible. So indeed they are in evolution—one can either stay still and be classical, academic and null, or go forward. But at a time of revolution it is not possible to stay still, one must either go forward, or back. To us this choice appears as a choice between Communism and Fascism, either to create the future or to go back to old primitive values, to mythology, racialism, nationalism, hero-worship, and *participation mystique*. This Fascist art is like the regression of the neurotic to a previous level of adaptation.

It is Lawrence's importance as an artist that he was well aware of the fact that the pure artist cannot exist to-day, and that the artist must inevitably be a man hating cash relationships and the market, and profoundly interested in the relations between persons. Moreover, he must be a man not merely profoundly interested in the relations between persons as they are, but interested in changing them, dissatisfied with them as they are, and wanting newer and fuller values in personal relationships.

But it is Lawrence's final tragedy that his solution was ultimately Fascist and not Communist. It was regressive. Lawrence wanted us to return to the past, to the 'Mother'. He sees human discontent as the yearning of the solar plexus for the umbilical connexion, and he demands the substitution for sharp sexual love of the unconscious fleshy identification of foetus with mother. All this was symbolic of regression, of neurosis, of the return to the primitive.

Lawrence felt that the Europe of to-day was moribund ; and he turned therefore to other forms of existence, in Mexico, Etruria and Sicily, where he found or thought he found systems of social relations in which life flowed more easily and more meaningfully. The life of Bourgeois Europe seemed to him permeated with possessiveness and rationalising, so that it had got out of gear with the simple needs of the body. In a thousand forms he repeats this indictment of a civilisation which consciously *and just because it is conscious*—sins against the instinctive currents which are man's primal source of energy. It is a mistake to suppose that Lawrence preaches the gospel of sex. Bourgeois Europe has had its bellyful of sex, and a sex cult would not now attract the interest and emotional support which Lawrence's teaching received. Lawrence's gospel was purely sociological. Even sex was too conscious for him.

'Anybody who calls my novel (Lady Chatterley's Lover) a dirty sexual novel, is a liar. It's not even a sexual novel : it's a phallic. Sex is a thing that exists in the head, its reactions are cerebral, and its processes mental. Whereas the phallic reality is warm and spontaneous——'

Again he wrote :

'What ails me is the absolute frustration of my primitive societal instinct . . . I think societal instinct much deeper than the sex instinct—and societal repression much more devastating. There is no repression of the sexual individual comparable to the repression of the societal man in me, by the individual ego, my own and everybody else's. I am weary even of my own individuality, and simply nauseated by other people's.'

One more analysis by him of the evil in bourgeois culture : (In the Cornish people)—

'the old race is still revealed, a race which believed in the darkness, in magic, and in the magic transcendency of one man over another which is fascinating. Also there is left some of the old sensuousness of the darkness and warmth and passionateness of the blood, sudden, incalculable. Whereas they are like insects, gone cold, living only for money, for *dirt*. They are foul in this. They ought to die.'

Now here is a clear artistic, i.e. *emotional*, analysis of the decay of bourgeois social relations. They live for money, the societal instinct is repressed, even the sex relations have become cold and infected. Survivals of barbaric social relations between men (the 'magic transcendency' of man over man) stand out as valuable in a culture where these relations have become relations between man and a thing, *man and dirt.*

But Lawrence does not look for a cause in social relations themselves, but in man's consciousness of them. The solution of the individual's needs is then plainly to be found in a return to instinctive living. But how are we to return to instinctive living? By casting off consciousness; we must return along the path we have come. But intellectualism consists in this, that we give either linguistically, plastically, or mentally, a symbolic projection to portions of reality, and consciousness or thinking consists simply in shuffling these images or verbal products. If therefore we are to cast off intellectualism and consciousness we must abandon all symbolism and rationalisation *tout court*, we must *be*, and no longer think, even in images. Yet on the contrary Lawrence again and again *consciously* formulates his creed in intellectual terms or terms of imagery. But this is self-contradiction, for how can we be led intellectually and consciously *back* from consciousness? It is our consciousness that Lawrence attempts to extend and heighten even at the moment he urges us to abandon it.

Consciousness can only be abandoned in action, and the first action of Fascism is the crushing of culture and the burning of the books. It is impossible therefore for an artist and thinker to be a consistent Fascist. He can only be like Lawrence, a self-contradictory one, who appeals to the consciousness of men to abandon consciousness.

There is a confusion here due to equating consciousness with thinking and unconsciousness with feeling.

This is wrong. Both are conscious. No one ever had or could have an unconscious affect or emotion. Feeling indeed is what makes the unconscious memory-traces conscious, and heats them into thoughts. All of us, in times of deep feeling, whether artistic or emotional feeling, are aware of heightened consciousness almost like a white light in us so intense and clear is it. But Lawrence never clearly saw this, and constantly equates unconsciousness with feeling and consciousness with intellect. For example :

'My great religion is a belief in the blood, in the flesh, as being wiser than the intellect. We can go wrong in our minds. But what our blood feels and believes and says is always true. The intellect is only a bit and a bridle. What do I care about knowledge? All I want is to answer to my blood, direct, without fumbling intervention of mind, or moral, or what not. I conceive a man's body as a kind of flame, like a candle flame forever upright and yet flowing : and the intellect is just the light that is shed on the things around, coming God knows how from out of practically nowhere, and being *itself*, whatever there is around it that it lights up. We have got so ridiculously mindful, that we never know that we ourselves are anything—we think there are only the objects we shine upon. And there the poor flame goes on burning ignored, to produce this light. And instead of chasing the mystery in the fugitive, half-lighted things outside us, we ought to look at ourselves and say, " My God,

I am myself!" That is why I like to live in Italy. The people are so unconscious. They only feel and want, they don't know. We know too much. No, we only *think* we know such a lot. A flame isn't a flame because it lights up two, or twenty objects on a table. It's a flame because it is itself. And we have forgotten ourselves.'

Feeling and thinking play into each other's hands and heighten each other. Man feels more deeply than the slug because he thinks more. Why did Lawrence make this error of supposing them essentially exclusive, and equate feeling with unconsciousness? Once again, the answer is in the nature of current society. All feeling and all thinking must contain something of each other to form part of consciousness at all. But it is possible to distinguish certain conscious phenomena as chiefly feeling, or vice versa. 'Pure' feelings, any more than 'Pure' thoughts, do not exist at all, since the first would be a mere instinctive tendency, the second nothing but a mnemic trace. Both would be unconscious and evidenced therefore only in behaviour. Lawrence might mean that feeling has wilted under modern conditions and that we must expand the feeling basis of our consciousness.

We know this of feelings (and affects generally) that they come into consciousness associated with innate responses or—more loosely—that they seem to be born of the modification, by experience and in action of the 'instincts'. Instinct going out in unmodified action, in mechanical response to a stimulus, is without *feeling*, it is pure automatism. Only when it becomes modified by memory traces or stifled by action does it become conscious and appear as feeling. The more intelligent the animal, the more its behaviour is modifiable by experience, the more feeling it displays. This extra display of feeling is *because* it is more intelligent, more conscious, less swayed by heredity, more subject to personal experience. Modification of innate responses by experience simply implies that previous behaviour leaves a mnemic trace on the neurones, chiefly of the cortex. These when innervated produce a new pattern, whose modification takes in the cortical sphere the form of thoughts and, in the visceral and thalamic sphere, the form of feelings or emotional dynamism. The different proportion of the components decides whether we call them thoughts or feelings. Even the simplest thought is irradiated with affect, and even the simplest emotion is accompanied by a thought, not necessarily verbalised but of some such character as 'I am hurt', or 'A pain'. It is because thought and feeling arise from the same modification of innate responses, by experience, that the growth of intelligence, i.e. of the *capacity* for modification of behaviour by experience, is accompanied by a steadily increasing emotional complexity, richness, and deepness. It is plain that the growth of civilisation in *Homo Sapiens* has been accompanied by a steady increase in sensibility to pain and pleasure. This is the famous 'sensitiveness' of civilised man, the 'luxury' of high cultures, which is also manifested in their art and their vocabulary. Primitive peoples on the other hand show a marked deficiency in their sensibility, not only to refined emotions but even the cruder ones. The extremely erotic character of savage dances is not due, as some observers naïvely suppose, to the emotional erethism of the natives, but to the reverse, that in them the erotic impulses, owing to their deficient sensibility, can only be aroused by violent stimulation, whereas a slight stimulus will set off the hair-trigger emotions of civilised people. The same phenomenon is shown in primitive insensibility to pain. Consequently if we are to return down the path we have come from, back to primitiveness, to the blood, to the flesh, it is not only to less and cruder thought but also to less and cruder feeling, to a lessened consciousness in which feeling and thought, precisely because they are less rich and complex, will be more intimately mingled, until finally, as they both blend completely and become one, they vanish and nothing is left but unconscious *behaviour*. But how can this goal be of value to an artist, save on condition he denies himself the very law of his being? Art is not unconscious behaviour, it is conscious feeling.

It is, however, possible to broaden feeling without altering thought or losing consciousness, by altering the ratio between them in modern civilisation. That is precisely the purpose of art, for the artist makes use always of just those verbal or pictorial images of reality which are more charged with feeling than cognition, and he organises them in such a way that the affects re-inforce each other and fuse to a glowing mass. Consequently, he who believes that at all costs the feeling element must be broadened in present-day consciousness, must preach and secure, not the contraction of all consciousness, but the widening of feeling consciousness. This is art's mission. Art is the technique of affective manipulation in relation to reality. Lawrence was doing what I suppose him to have wished to do, just when he was artist pure and simple, sensitively recording the spirit of a place or the emotions of real people—in his early work. In proportion as he became a prophet, preaching a gospel intellectually, he departed from that goal.

How did he come to make first the initial *sortie* in favour of feeling, and then the contradictory error, deserting art for preaching ? He came to the first conclusion because feeling is impoverished by modern bourgeois culture. Social relations, by ceasing to be between man and man and adhering to a thing, become emptied of tenderness. Man feels himself deprived of love. His whole instinct revolts against this. He feels a vast maladaption to his environment. Lawrence perceives this clearly when he talks about the repression of the societal instinct.

But things have gone so far that no tinkering with social relations, no adaptation of the instincts to the environment by means of art, will cure this. Social relations themselves must be rebuilt. The artist is bound for the sake of his integrity to become thinker and revolutionary. Lawrence therefore was bound not to be content with pure art, with widening feeling consciousness in the old circle. He had to try and recast social relations and proceed to a solution. But there is only one revolutionary solution. Social relations must be altered, not so as to contract consciousness but so as to widen it. The higher feeling must be found, not in a lower but as always in a higher level of culture.

Naturally consciousness seems in bourgeois culture now, as in all periods of decay, full of defects with which being struggles, and this seems like unconsciousness crippled by consciousness. Those defects in bourgeois social relations all arise from the cash nexus which replaces all other social ties, so that society seems held together, not by mutual love or tenderness or obligation, but simply by profit. Money makes the bourgeois world go round and this means that selfishness is the hinge on which bourgeois society turns, for money is a dominating relation to an owned thing. This commercialisation of all social relations invades the most intimate of emotions, and the relations of the sexes are affected by the differing economic situations of man and woman. The notion of private property, aggravated by its importance and overwhelming power in bourgeois relations, extends to love itself. Because economic relations in capitalism are simply each man struggling for himself in the impersonal market, the world seems torn apart with the black forces of envy, covetousness and hate, which mix with and make ambivalent even the most 'altruistic' emotions.

But it is simplifying the drama to make it a struggle between contemporary consciousness and old being. It is a conflict between productive relations and productive powers, between the contemporary formulations of consciousness, and all the possibilities of future being including consciousness latent in society and struggling to be released from their bonds. Bourgeois defects are implicit in bourgeois civilisation and therefore in bourgeois consciousness. Hence man wants to turn against the intellect, for it seems that the intellect is his enemy, and indeed it is, if by intellect we mean the bourgeois intellect. But it can only be fought with intellect. To deny intellect is to assist the forces of conservatism. In hundreds of diverse forms we see to-day the useless European revolt against intellectualism.

In any civilisation the rôle of consciousness is to modify instinctive responses so that they flow smoothly into the mill of social relations and turn it. Instinct not money really turns the social mill, though in the bourgeois world instinctive relations can only operate along the money channel. Hence when social relations come to be a brake on society's forces, there is felt a conflict between the social relations and the instincts. It seems as if the feelings were out of gear, as if the world was uncomfortable and hurt the feelings and repressed them. It seems as if the instincts, and the feelings, those products of the instincts, were being penalised by the environment, and that, therefore, the instincts and feelings must be 'given their due', must be exalted even if it means breaking up and abandoning the civilised environment for a more primitive one. To-day this exaltation of the instincts is seen in all demands for a return to deeper 'feeling' as with Lawrence, and in all worships of unconscious 'mentation', as with the surréalists, Hemingways, and Fascists. In individuals this mechanism is infantile regression, seen in its pathological form in the neuroses.

Now these mechanisms involve the discovery of a real defect. Social being *is* held back by social consciousness; the instincts *are* thwarted and the feelings *are* made poor by the environment. But the remedy is wrong. The neurotic cannot, as we know, be cured by infantile regression. All it does for him is to secure him unconsciousness and take from him painful thoughts, at the price of a lowering of consciousness and an impoverishing of values. Civilisation cannot be cured by going back along the path to the primitive, it can only become at a lower level more unconscious of its decay. Just as the neurotic's return to childhood solutions of problems is unhealthier than childhood, so a civilisation's return to a primitive solution is unhealthier than primitive life itself. The very history between makes such solutions unreal. To the primitive these problems have never existed. To the regressive they have existed but he has repressed them. It is into the wilderness these people would lead us. They preach, not new vigour, but old decadence.

What then is the cure? We know that both in the case of the neurotic and the civilisation, the cure is a more strenuous and creative act than the invalid's relapse into the womb of that unconsciousness from which we emerged. Our task is to be performed, not in an air heavy and fetid with mysteries and dead symbolism like that of a cavern used for old obscene rites, but in the open air.

We are not to return to the old but it is into the new we must go; and the new does not exist, we must bring it into being. The child would love to return to the womb, but it must become adult and face the strenuous and bracing tasks of life. We are not to abandon consciousness but to expand it, to deepen and purge feeling and break up and recast thought, and this new consciousness does not exist in any thing's keeping either Mexicans or Yogis or the 'blood' but we must make it ourselves. In this struggle with reality in which instincts, feeling and thought all partake and interact, the instincts themselves will be changed, and emerging in consciousness as new thought and new feeling, will once again feel themselves in harmony with the new environment they have created. Social relations must be changed so that love returns to the earth and man is not only wiser but more full of emotion. This is not a task which one prophet can perform in one Gospel, but since the whole fabric of social relations are to be changed, every human being must in some sort participate in the change, be either for it or against it, and be victorious if he is for it and be defeated if he is against it.

Why did Lawrence, faced with the problem, fail of a solution? He failed because while hating bourgeois culture he never succeeded in escaping from its limitations. Here in him, too, we see the same old lie. Man is 'free' in so far as his 'free' instincts, the 'blood', the 'flesh', are given an outlet. Man is free not through but *in spite of* social relations.

If one believes this—which, as we have seen, is the deepest and most ineradicable bourgeois illusion, all others are built on this—one must, if one is hurt by bourgeois social relations, see security and freedom only in casting them off, and returning to a primitive state with less 'constraints'. One must necessarily believe freedom and happiness can be found by one's own individual action. One will not believe freedom and happiness can only be found through social relations, by co-operating with others to change them, but there is always something one can do, fly to Mexico, find the right woman or the right friends, and so discover salvation. One will never see the truth, that one can only find salvation for oneself by finding it for all others at the same time.

Lawrence therefore could never escape from this essential selfishness—not a petty selfishness but the selfishness which is the pattern of bourgeois culture and is revealed in pacifism, Protestantism, and all varieties of salvation obtained by individual action.

The world to which Lawrence wished to return is not really the world of primitives who are in fact bound by more rigid relations than those of bourgeois Europe. It is the old bourgeois pastoral heaven of the 'natural man' born everywhere in chains, which does not exist. It does not exist because it is self-contradictory, and because it is self-contradictory the bourgeois world in striving for it more clearly produces the opposite, as in moving towards an object in a mirror we move away from the real object. Lawrence's gospel therefore only forms part of the self-destructive element in bourgeois culture.

Lawrence for all his gifts suffered from the old *petit bourgeois* errors. Like Wells, he strove to climb upwards into the world of bourgeois culture; being more artistic than Wells and born in a later era, it could not be the security and power of that already sick class that appealed to him. It was their cultural values. He succeeded in entering that world and drinking deeply of all its tremendous intellectual and æsthetic riches, only to find them riches turning into dust. The shock of that disillusion, added to the pain endured in that climb, filled him finally with a hatred for bourgeois values. He could criticise them relentlessly and bitterly, but he could provide no solution for the whole set of his life; all that long difficult climb of his into the bourgeois sunshine ensured that he remained a bourgeois. His was always bourgeois culture, conscious of its decay, criticising itself and with no solution except to go back to a time when things were different and so undo all the development that had brought bourgeois culture to this pass.

Had he been born later, had that sunlit world never appealed to him so irresistibly, he might have seen that it was the proletariat—to whom he was so near at the start of his climb—that was the dynamic force of the future. Not only would he then have had a standpoint outside bourgeois culture from which to criticise it, but from that position he would have been able to find the true solution—in the future, not the past. But Lawrence remained to the end a man incapable of that subordination of self to others, of co-operation, of solidarity as a class, which is the characteristic of the proletariat. He remained the individualist, the bourgeois revolutionary angrily working out his own salvation, critical of all, alone in possession of grace. He rid himself of every bourgeois illusion but the important one. He saw finally neither the world nor himself as it really was. He saw the march of events as a bourgeois tragedy, which is true but unimportant. The important thing, which was absolutely closed to him, was that it was also a proletarian renaissance.

Everywhere to-day will be found the conscious or unconscious followers of Lawrence—the pacifists, the snug little hedonists, the conscientious sexualists, the well-meaning Liberals, the idealists, all seeking the impossible solution, salvation through the free act of the individual will amid decay and disaster. They may find a temporary solution, a momentary happiness, although I judge Lawrence to have found neither.

But it is of its nature unstable, for external events to which they have regressively adjusted themselves, beget incessantly new horrors and undreamed-of disasters. What avails such pinchbeck constructs during the screaming horror of a War? One may stop one's ears and hide oneself in Cornwall like Lawrence, but the cry of one's millions of suffering fellow-humans reaches one's ears and tortures one. And, the War at last survived, there come new horrors. The eating disintegration of the slump. Nazism outpouring a flood of barbarism and horror. And what next? Armaments piling up like an accumulating catastrophe, mass neurosis, nations like mad dogs. All this seems gratuitous, horrible, cosmic to such people, unaware of the causes. How can the bourgeois still pretend to be free, to find salvation individually? Only by sinking himself in still cruder illusions, by denying art, science, emotion, even ultimately life itself. Humanism, the creation of bourgeois culture, finally separates from it. Against the sky stands Capitalism without a rag to cover it, naked in its terror. And humanism, leaving it, or rather, forcibly thrust aside, must either pass into the ranks of the proletariat or, going quietly into a corner, cut its throat. Lawrence did not live to face this final issue, which would necessarily make straw of his philosophy and his teaching.

IV

H. G. WELLS

A STUDY IN UTOPIANISM

'*The Utopian's mode of thought has for a long time governed the socialist ideas of the nineteenth century and still governs some of them. Until very recently all French and English Socialists did homage to it. . . . To all these, Socialism is the expression of absolute truth, reason, and justice, and has only to be discovered to conquer all the world by virtue of its own power. And as absolute truth is independent of time, space, and of the historical development of man, it is a mere accident when and where it is discovered. With all this, absolute truth, reason, and justice are different with the founder of each different school. And as each one's special kind of absolute truth, reason, and justice is again conditioned by his subjective understanding, his conditions of existence, the measure of his knowledge and his intellectual training, there is no other ending possible in this conflict of absolute truths than that they shall be mutually exclusive one of the other. Hence, from this can come nothing but a kind of eclectic, average Socialism, which, as a matter of fact, has up to the present time dominated the minds of most of the Socialist workers in France and England. Hence, a mish-mash allowing of the most manifold shades of opinion ; a mish-mash of such critical statements, economic theories, pictures of future society by the founders of different sects, as excite a minimum of opposition ; a mish-mash which is the more easily brewed the more the definite sharp edges of the individual constituents are rubbed down in the stream of debate, like rounded pebbles in a brook.'*

ENGELS : 'SOCIALISM—UTOPIAN AND SCIENTIFIC.'

IT is evident that long before H. G. Wells had become famous as a writer, Marx's collaborator, in the analysis quoted above, had accurately characterised Wells's Utopianism. Engels was interested, not only in the phenomenon presented by each Utopian socialist who feels that he knows to the last detail what the world ought to be, but in how when these Utopian socialists, each with their precise but widely differing ideas, attempt to co-operate in any way, nothing can result but a general cloudy vagueness inhibiting action. This mixture, as Engels said, is a mish-mash.

The peculiarity of H. G. Wells, however, and the point in which he, as a later development of the school, differs from the earlier Utopian socialists Engels referred to, is in that he is not just one of the contributors to a mish-mash but the mish-mash itself. This was inevitable. Wells's muddled thinking is not due, as he naïvely suggests in his *Experiment in Autobiography*, to some peculiarity of the blood supply to his brain, but to the anarchy of the world in which he was born. To early Utopian socialists the world was something precise, for bourgeois values were still precise. Equality, freedom and democracy were concepts that seemed to have meaning. How can they now, when equality has in some strange way become domination by trust capital, freedom is wage-slavery and democracy is Fascist Imperialism ?

The Utopian socialists' absolute liberty, freedom, etc., were the bourgeois values of their time, hypostatised as eternal. So are Wells's. But in Engels's time these values were not changing so rapidly as to be transformed into their opposites almost overnight. In Wells's time this is just what has happened. And so each year sees Wells and those like him with a different Utopia and a new world-view. Wells is in the unhappy position of a tailor whose yard-rule alters capriciously in length overnight. Each morning he patiently measures off his yard of cloth, and the result is a long succession of inconsistent bundles of material. With each new book Wells sees Utopias run on new principles ; new forms of salvation for man ; new secret diseases accounting for present discontents ; new Gods, invisible Kings. It is the unreason of it all that sickens Wells. If only man would be reasonable. Yet surely man can hardly be blamed for not trusting to reason if, in Wells's hands, it produces so many diverse solutions, from a universal world-democratic federation to a world run by Samurai-bosses, from Liberal Fascism to a Roosevelt Brain Trust, from an open conspiracy to a world saved by a war so ghastly it destroys civilisation. Surely, rather than trust to the yard-stick of Wells's ideology, it would be better to go on measuring out the material in the old Victorian bourgeois way. Other men have their separate standards of absolute truth, reason and justice, according to the different parts of the bourgeois system in which they find themselves, and Wells's absolutely just and reasonable Utopias do not appeal to them at all. To God-fearing folk the morals of some of Mr. Wells's Utopias seem most unjust. To the dress trade the nudity of *Men Like Gods* appears far from divine. Business men consider that scientists are unduly important in these States of to-morrow. Even those whose conceptions of the absolute are quite as simple and *petit bourgeois* as those of Wells, cannot fight down an uneasy feeling that the perfectly just, happy and beautiful State he paints would be unutterably boring.

For Wells is a *petit bourgeois*, and of all the products of capitalism, none is more unlovely than this class. Whoever does not escape from it is certainly damned. It is necessarily a class whose whole existence is based on a lie. Functionally it is exploited, but because it is allowed to share in some of the crumbs of exploitation that fall from the rich bourgeois table, it identifies itself with the bourgeois system on which, whether as bank manager, small shopkeeper or upper household servant, it seems to depend. It has only one value in life, that of bettering itself, of getting a step nearer the good bourgeois things so far above it. It has only one horror, that of falling from respectability into the proletarian abyss which, because it is so near, seems so much more dangerous. It is rootless, individualist, lonely, and perpetually facing, with its hackles up, an antagonistic world. It can never know the security of the rich bourgeoisie or the companionship of the worker. It can never rest on anything, for it is always struggling to better itself. It is the most deluded class, for it has not the cynicism of the worker with practical proof of bourgeois fictions, or the cynicism of the intelligent bourgeois who even while he maintains them for his own purposes sees through the illusions of religion, royalty, patriotism and capitalist 'industry' and 'foresight'. It has no traditions of its own and it does not adopt those of the workers, which it hates, but those of the bourgeois, which are without virtue for it, since it did not help to create them. This world, described so well in *Experiment in Autobiography*, is like a terrible stagnant marsh, all mud and bitterness, and without even the saving grace of tragedy.

Everyone seeks to escape from this marsh. It is a world whose whole motive force is simply this, to escape from what it was born to, upwards, to be rich, secure, a boss. And the development of capitalism increases the depth of this world, makes wealth, security, and freedom more and more difficult, and thus adds to its horror. More and more the petty bourgeois expression is that of a face lined with petty, futile, bewildered discontent. Life with its perplexities and muddles seems to baffle and betray them at every turn. They are frustrated, beaten; things are too much for them. Almost all Wells's characters from Kipps to Clissold are psychologically of this typical *petit bourgeois* frustrated class. They can never understand why everything is so puzzling, why man is so unreasonable, why life is so difficult, precisely because it is they who are so unreasonable. They are born of the irresponsibility and anachronism of capital expressed in its acutest form. And they do not understand this.

The ways of escape from the *petit bourgeois* world are many. One way is to shed one's false bourgeois illusions and relapse into the proletarian hell one has always dreaded. Then one finds a life hard and laborious enough but with clear values, derived from the functional part one plays in society. The peculiarly dreadful flavour of *petit bourgeois* bitterness is gone, for now the social forces that produce unhappiness—unemployment, poverty and privation—come quite clearly from above, from outside, from an alien world. One encounters them as members of a class, as companions in misfortune, and this generates both the sympathy and the organisation that makes them easier to be sustained. 'It's the poor what helps the poor.' The proletariat are called upon to hate, not each other but impersonal things like wars and slumps and booms, or classes outside themselves—the bosses, the rich.

It is the peculiar suffering of the *petit bourgeoisie* that they are called upon to hate *each other*. It is not impersonal things or *outside* classes that hurt them and inflict on them suffering and poverty, but it appears to be other members of their own class. It is the shopkeeper across the road, the rival small trader, the family next door, with whom they are actively competing. Every success of one *petit bourgeois* is a sword in another's heart. Every failure of one's own is the result of another's activity. No companionship, or solidarity, is possible. One's hatred extends from the workers 'below' that abyss always waiting for one, to the successful *petit bourgeois* just above one whom one envies and hates.

The development of capitalism increases both trends, the solidarity of the workers and the dissension and bitterness of the *petit bourgeoisie*.

It is also possible to escape upwards. Many are called. All who do not sink into the proletariat strive upwards. Only a few are chosen. Only a few struggle into the ranks of the rich bourgeoisie. Wells was one of those few. The story of this sharp, fierce struggle and its ultimate success in terms of his bank passbook is recorded in Wells's Autobiography.

Some try to escape into the world of art or pure thought. But this 'escape' becomes increasingly difficult. Take the case of the artist in the young Wells's position. A dominating interest in art will come to him perhaps as an interest in poetry, in the short story, in new novelist's technique. Painful and unproductive at first, his study of his craft will also be uneconomic. It will not pay. But how is he to live? Is he to proletarianise himself? Is he to starve in a garret on poor relief? But starvation in a garret as an outcast 'despised' member of the community will necessarily condition his whole outlook as an artist. He will write reacting with or against proletarianisation, or as an unsuccessful petty bourgeois, or as an enforced member of the *lumpen-*

proletariat, and all society will seem compulsive, rotten and inimical to him. Moreover, art itself in that era, being the aggregate of art produced by these and their like antecedent conditions, will be more and more outcast, turned in on itself, non-functional, and subjective, it will be the sincere, decadent, anarchistic art of a Picasso or Joyce.

It was impossible for Wells, imbued with this burning desire, to escape from the petty bourgeois hell, to accept art as an avocation, a social rôle, and be driven in on himself as an outcast from bourgeois values. He could only accept it as a means to success and the best road to cash. His autobiography reveals the early stages of his struggles in the literary market to attain five-figure sales and a five-figure income.

It is probable that Wells had, naturally, a primarily artistic bent. His gift for vivid metaphor and the word used with a delight in its texture appears in welcome flashes amid oceans of turgid and shoddy thinking. But once having denied art as an avocation justified by its social utility in favour of art as a cash-producer justified by sales, the development of his writer's gift was stifled. No characters live in his novels except as transitory aspects of himself. The conflicts of his characters are unreal, their relationships unconvincing and non-progressive, the whole background and action is pervaded by a superficiality and shoddiness which Henry James analysed correctly. Wells has not created any art of importance, and his life spent in the petty bourgeois upward struggle has prevented him from getting into touch with reality. No real contemporary problem is ever the theme of his novels. Doubtless this explains the appeal to his mind of the scientific fantasy, with which alone—and then only in his youth—he achieves any measure of artistic success.

There was also the escape into the world of 'pure' thought. But the scientist is faced with the same kind of problem as the artist, although only now has it become as acute. One can fasten oneself to thought, but then how, speculating, is one to live by speculating? The problem will affect one's thought, by one's isolation and inability to obtain the apparatus and assistance for experiments.

Alternatively one can find work as a thinker and bring one's scientific capabilities to the cash market. Here bourgeoisdom is kinder to science than to art, for science is more often profitable to it. There are posts where the thinker is paid merely to think. But these are few and already growing fewer. Most scientists must live on patents, armament research, and teaching. Bourgeoisdom warns them severely that science is growing a nuisance; there is over-production, 'there should be a close period for invention'.

As it happened, Wells tried this way of escape also. He studied under Huxley. Rightly or wrongly, he believes he would have made a good scientist. But once again the necessity of escaping from petty bourgeois poverty stepped in. He became a demonstrator in order to be able to afford to marry, and presently was writing articles for the popular press. His possible scientific career was blocked by the necessity of 'keeping up' a wife and home.

But these experiences of his in his escape into wealth, necessarily taught him all the difficulties and all the frustrations of his class in their acutest form. His books are full of pity for the typical *petit bourgeois*—'poor dear muddled' So-and-so, solitary, discontented, ambitious, subject to blind forces. He is unable to overcome his *petit bourgeois* reverence for the big bourgeois—the Roosevelt, the far-seeing capitalist visualised as a *Samurai*. And he is unable even to imagine what workers are like: As he acknowledges, he does not know them, has not talked to them, cannot understand them. All he has of them is childhood memories of the proletarian abyss below the *petit bourgeois*, the dreadful Morlocks whom one must kill blindly when revolting they come up to the light of day.

This means that Wells's world is unreal. The whole world of modern society derives its energy and character from the interplay between the bourgeois and the workers. The *petit bourgeoisie*, the only class Wells understands, is simply the dust flung off by the impact of these two forces. Therefore it is impossible for him to grasp what is happening in the world to-day. Everything seems mysterious, arbitrary, frustrated. But because he has climbed into bourgeois security he must always without realising what he is doing identify himself with bourgeois interests. He must crusade for Imperialism in the War, for liberal Fascism and a New Deal during peace. He must always loathe all signs of the arising of the Morlocks, and crusade relentlessly against Marx or any Socialism that admits the existence of classes, that is 'ungracious' or 'bitter'. Classes are mere fictions, he tells us, due to our deluding ourselves with 'personæ' and myths. Thus Wells understands the world less than the crudest hard-fisted capitalist, who knows clearly what he stands for and with whom he is fighting.

Since contemporary conditions not only hurt and frustrated Wells in his upwards struggle from the *petit bourgeoisie,* but forced him also to trample on such longings as he may have had for art or science, Wells necessarily took a critical attitude towards these conditions, and equally necessarily, because he did not understand them, could only criticise them with irresponsibility and constantly changing opinions. He took the rôle of popular 'thinker', writer of the novel 'of ideas' and of 'outlines' of science and history, because he had been unable to pursue real art and had been forced to forsake real science. He could not be creative, for creation is the prerogative of the man who is real artist or real scientist. Necessarily therefore he became the great *entrepreneur* of modern and not-so-modern theories. Although lately science and history have left him behind, he was able to use all the discoveries of, say, 1890 to 1910—psycho-analysis, early anthropology and comparative religion, archæology, physics and biology. But because he was devoid of any world-view and had not escaped from the inborn bewilderment of the *petit bourgeois,* he can make nothing but a muddle of all these ideas—an eclectic mish-mash. The subtlest and acutest hypothesis in his hands somehow becomes clumsy and shoddy. Science's most vital discoveries recounted by him seem grey and linen-draperish. Can there ever have been a man accepted seriously as a thinker, who showed so little capacity not merely for original but even for clear and logical thought? Wells might have occupied a position similar to that of the Encyclopædists. But the Encyclopædists were bourgeois in an age of bourgeois revolution. They belonged to the dynamic force of society. They were part of its structure, one of the vital levers in the machine, not like Wells part of what is not even a dying class but the fluff broken off that class in its operation. Therefore these Encyclopædists had a perfectly clear and definite world-view. It was a real world they lived in, and whose structure they knew from inside. All the contemporary discoveries they popularised were fitted into a coherent real frame. Wells had nothing in which to fit them; hence the characteristic Wellsian muddle.

It is a strange and in a way pathetic illusion this of Wells, that by forsaking art, science and action for 'propaganda', he can change the world. We can see its genesis, how it arose necessarily from the circumstances of his ascent from the *petit bourgeois* hell and his abandonment of science and art. It takes shape in the typical bourgeois error, the error that thought is prior and moves the world and that if only people would see reason (while the capitalist machine remorsely constrains their every movement) they would act rightly.

Wells sees—as must every man of even normal intelligence, and Wells is a man of more than that—on the one hand the hopeless confusion of bourgeois social relations, and on the other hand that society's productive forces, in the form of physics (science) and machinery (technical resources), contain enormous potency which can only be realised in different social relations.

But the proletariat does not exist for Wells. The change therefore can only come from within the bourgeois class. The task of ' setting right ' the world becomes one of showing the bourgeoisie their errors. The world is to be set right by argument. But the very fact that he thinks this indicates that he himself has no rational basis on which to argue, that he is intellectually one with those he wishes to convert. He does not see that the principle of causality involves that bourgeois social relations have not only given birth to enormous powers and the possibility of their own destruction, but also to all the irrationalities of ideology which reflect the same confusion. He assumes on the contrary that the concepts lying naturally in his mind were not formed by his education and his environment, but are God-given concepts of absolute justice and truth, a spark of the undying fire. He supposed instead that the muddle-headedness, ignorance, blindness, wickedness, wastefulness, and militancy of men that he saw around him had produced the muddled world of economic, politic, and social relations, as if men had not been born with blank minds and educated in the world but had stepped suddenly on the earth and by a fiat of their wills had produced the sad picture. It is the old bourgeois error of knowing producing being, of the freedom and primacy of thought. As always, man's will is believed free in itself, and not only in so far as it creates conditions which realise its freedom. The historical outline which made Wells famous is not defective, as bourgeois historians assert, because of its neglect of this or that fact, its minor inaccuracies, its cavalier treatment of 'great men', its 'new' interpretation of policies. On the contrary, never was a better miniature bourgeois history written than this Outline. There are no classes. Wars are caused by men's identification of themselves with tribal gods such as Britannia and Kathleen in Houlihan. The Outline is notable for its complete lack of any causal presentation of historical development, so that man's enthralling and noble history, so rich in content, so tense with effort, so perpetually new in quality and process, seems nothing but a nightmare of ideological futility, in which unreasonable kings and unscientific statesmen and well-meaning religious leaders lead their unfortunate followers in a will-o'-the-wisp dance—a gloomy scene, relieved only by the shrill voice of Wells's angry preaching.

Wells makes the old bourgeois assumption that men are born, each perfectly free, and that their wants and dreams mould the world of social relations, not that the world of social relations their wants and dreams, which in turn react upon the world of social relations to produce a continual process of historical development. Because of this Wells naturally makes the 'logical' deduction that to change man's mind it is necessary to preach to them convincingly and interestingly, and then all will be accomplished as one desires. Moreover, since he assumes that the relation between mind and environment is perfectly fluid, that the mind can make of the environment anything it pleases, he quite logically considers as his primary task the drawing up of a completely planned Utopia, including details of drainage, morals, and election methods, so that this planned Utopia can by his converted readers be brought into being. And because this Utopia is planned in minute detail, according to the best ideals of the bourgeoisie on the particular day on which he is writing, he has the ludicrous illusion that this is scientific socialism and (actually) that Marxism is unscientific. Wells's 'science' requires as its first step the substitution for all laws of causality of the free operation of the mind, and it is characteristic of his completely bourgeois mentality that he does not see this and does not even understand the principles on which his theories are based. It is doubtful if Wells has ever realised, in spite of his scientific education, that the whole purpose of Marx was to write history causally. Social development may, as in the bourgeois world, be *apparently* governed by the blind forces of 'nature' producing slumps and wars, or as in communism it may be governed increasingly by the conscious and therefore planned forces of society; but in both cases there is a causal relation beneath phenomena. It is because the bourgeois denies causality as Wells does in his Outline, and because the Communist asserts it, and discovers its law, that man in communism can become free. To deny the existence of laws, as the savage denies the existence of physical causality by substituting mythology, is to be the slave of those laws. To assert or discover them, as does the scientist, is to be their master.

In these latter days Wells can see small hope for our troubled world. What hope can exist within the circle of the ideas that rule his mind—since they are bourgeois ideas? Only two alternatives exist to-day within the bourgeois class, collapse or Fascism, and both are ultimately the same. All Wells's Utopian dreams of the future turn more and more on these two alternatives—on the one hand a New Deal, a State run by Samurai, a giant ultra-Imperialistic democratic world-state as the result of an open conspiracy—on the other hand, as in the *Shape of Things to Come*, complete collapse with the vague faith that somehow in some unspecified way, in some remote corner, the problems have all been miraculously solved and a Redeemer arrives from this Utopia in a glittering aeroplane to put things right from above, like a divine bureaucrat.

In all these Utopias thought reveals its solitary poverty. Thought visualising the future and divorced from action, can do no more than project the disheartening poverty of the present into the richness of the future. These bourgeois dream-Utopias with their standardisations, their extinction of national distinctions so dear to the heart of human beings, their characterless, commercialised, hygienic, eugenic, Aryan-Fascist uniformity, not only do not allure us—they revolt our minds. If the future holds no more than this, we think, let civilisation die. They hold us back and discourage us, rather than urge us on. But the lesson of history tells us that it is not so. Thought is not here to be trusted. Thought is static so long as it treads only thought's round and, like a metaphysical logician, cannot bring to birth newness or greater complexity, but only a reshuffling of those elements it already held, given it aforetime by action in experience. It is action that is rich and creative ; being is perpetually contriving new patterns and higher complexities. Action is more mysterious than that unmysterious word mystery, more varied and enchanting than that Utopia which, like a Christian Paradise, either repeats the sensual delights of the present or takes refuge in negatives—'tongue cannot say or heart conceive'. Action is the process of development itself and brings into birth what our limited thoughts cannot to-day conceive, and by doing so makes possible those richer thoughts we would long to think but cannot, those dreams we only dream of having. Is thought then utterly vain, a chance iridescence on the seething tumult of the sea of being ? No, for thought *is* being, is a part of being, developed historically as part of action to aid that action which we regard as primary, which action in turn casts fresh light on being. At every stage thought must find issue from action and, with what it has learned from action, return to fresh thinking, which again goes out to fresh action. Thus the boundaries of the known and influenced world perpetually widen, while its image in consciousness perpetually deepens and grows in complexity. This is the law of development, not only of science but of all thought whatever. The function of thought is not to shuffle its stale concepts into some fresh might-have-been world and expect action to follow suit, but to probe deep into the world of being, lay bare its causal structure, and draw from that causal structure the possibilities of future being. Man has already done this with physics, where, by knowing the necessities of dead matter, we are free of them and can subdue them within the limits of those laws to our own will. The same baring of causal structure was performed by Marx in the sphere of society, where, by exposing the principal laws of motion of bourgeois social relations, he has shown how thought can follow the grain thus revealed. Thought following the grain of social relations can, by action, by social revolution, make man fully conscious of himself as a man and plan society to achieve his own freedom. Thus while the Utopians project their unsatisfied aspirations into the future and expect being to conform, how they know not, the scientific socialist is concerned to find what defect in contemporary social relations has given birth to his aspirations, and to what new system of social relations, generated step by step out of the present, this symptom points. But as for what this world will be when social relations no longer press on man blindly but he is truly free—how can we children of a collapsing world, in all the ruin wrought by our outworn social relations, ourselves *exactly* predict?

Thus thought by remembering its integrity with being, whereby thought acquires a history and change and returns on the rest of action to enrich and guide it, gains the power it possesses only in bourgeois theory and in bourgeois use seems not to possess. In bourgeois theory thought is free of necessity and in bourgeois practice is therefore helpless in the face of necessity. In Marxist theory thought is conscious of necessity and is therefore free. Wells, believing that thought and consciousness are prime movers, has spent his whole life in 'popularising' his absolute truth and justice, in making them bright and attractive and vivid and easily digestible. He has been read 'by millions', but simply because of that his work has been a vain beating of the wind, for his very appeal to millions resulted from this, that his readers like himself were caught in the same round of bourgeois metaphysics, of thought eternally returning on itself and finding no outlet in action or connexion with reality. Yet Marx, who made no concessions to popular appeal and never attempted to make his doctrine 'attractive', who preached the subservience of thought to social necessity and wasted no time in planning beautiful Utopias—it is this Marx who appears to have shaken the bourgeois world. It is Marx's writing which appears to have overturned the government of one-sixth of a world and established a new order. It is Marx whose ideas in the remaining five-sixths are always the spear-point of social action and form the rallying point for the active forces of revolution in all countries. No one has moved into action behind the banner of Wells. If indeed thought alone moves the world 'of its own right' independent of its connexion with being, how is it that Marx's ideas, explained with so little 'propaganda', such lack of emotional appeal, prettiness and fantasy, so destitute of poetry and sex-appeal, appear to have conquered reality? All unconsciously, a bourgeois critic of Marx has grasped the truth. Marx, he said, has not produced revolutionary activity anywhere. It is the revival of revolutionary activity which has 'revived and reinflated' Marx. And this is true. The tremendous power of Marx's ideology is drawn, not from the form of that ideology but from the content of contemporary social relations. Marx, instead of voyaging into the future on a Time-Machine to find his own *petit bourgeois* ideas symbolised in Morlocks and Eloi, pierced into the heart of contemporary capitalist being and escaped from bourgeois ideology into the structure of bourgeois society. By exhibiting in his writings the causal laws he thus discovered, he also made possible the machinery of revolution which would change social relations by action, just as a scientist's discovery of a physical law permits the construction of machines to produce at will the phenomena generalised in the law. Marx's ideology has behind it all the pressure of the social forces of our age. Each slump, each war, every new business transaction, every concentration of capital, every fresh exploitation, every second of the development of bourgeois social relations, adds fresh force to the ideology of Marx, and as frosts break up a ground, prepares our minds, long tranced in the aridity of bourgeois thought, for the dawning consciousness of tomorrow.

It is Wells's tragedy that of all contemporaries who have interested themselves in social change and seen the anarchy of current social relations, he is least a Socialist and farthest from Marxism. And this, in its turn, is due to his *petit bourgeois* mind.

The bourgeois, as soon as he becomes disgusted with the muddle and decay of his own class, necessarily turns to the proletariat, and since he has only been taught to regard them as inferior brutes, he is able to turn to them with pity, as one turns to animals. He is able to regard them as the most suffering class, and this pity for the proletariat as the most suffering class burns brightly in the writings of Wassermann, Toller, Tolstoy, and Barbusse, and even warms faintly Shaw and Galsworthy. There is no trace of it in Wells, for Wells comes from a class that regards the proletariat not as passive inferior brutes but as something dirty and evil and dangerous and terribly near. Because he has been so busy getting upwards out of the petty bourgeois hell, Wells has never had time to become conscious of this limitation or learn the truth.

The conception of the proletariat as the most suffering class fills the disgusted bourgeois with indignation and passion. It becomes a source of emotion and humanity, well seen in Wassermann's *Christian Wahnschaffe*, that prevents such a man's writings from ever having the unreality or emotional aridity of Wells's.

They may burst into white flames of fury at the sufferings of the proletariat, as in Christian Wahnschaffe's cry to his father :

'The guilt that arises from what men do is small and scarcely comparable to the guilt that arises from what men fail to do. For what kinds of men are those, after all, who become guilty through their deeds? Poor, wretched, driven, desperate, half-mad creatures, who lift themselves up and bite the foot that treads them under. Yet they are made responsible and held guilty and punished with endless torments. But those who are guilty through failure in action are spared and are always secure, and have ready and reasonable subterfuges and excuses, yet they are, so far as I can see, the true criminals. All evil comes from them.'

Wells could never see his 'Morlocks' as Wassermann sees them, as 'poor, wretched, driven, desperate, half-mad creatures'. He could never burn with indignation and be restless at the thought of the proletariat 'Under Fire', exploited, transported to Siberia, always and everywhere the most suffering class.

And yet what leagues and leagues the bourgeois has yet to travel, even when arrived at this realisation of the proletariat as the most suffering class, before he can understand the reality of the society in which he finds himself! For he has to understand that this most suffering and exploited class, this herd of ill-treated animals, is something very different, the sole creative force of contemporary society. This class which he comes to comfort and set free and relieve, has on the contrary the task of comforting and releasing and reviving him. These sufferers afflicted by war and capitalist anarchy and slumps are to fight and destroy these very evils. The world of his youth whose ruins he sees tumbling on them, is to be rebuilt and more largely planned by them. This humiliating knowledge, which can only be won against his instincts, by an insight into the structure of the social relations in which he lives, is the most difficult of all wisdoms for the bourgeois to attain. Wells is a hundred miles from it. A long dispersed array of draggled pilgrims filed along the road to the revolution of thought and being. Only a few bourgeois have yet arrived there.

V

PACIFISM AND VIOLENCE

A STUDY IN BOURGEOIS ETHICS

THERE is not much left of importance in bourgeois ethics. Chastity, sobriety, salvation and cleanliness have ceased to be topics on which the bourgeois feels very deeply. There is, in fact, only one issue on which the bourgeois conscience is to-day warmed into activity. Pacifism, always latent in the bourgeois creed, has now crystallised out as almost the only emotionally-charged belief left in Protestant Christianity or in its analogue, bourgeois 'idealism'.

I call it a distinctively bourgeois doctrine, because I mean by pacifism, not the love of peace as a good to be secured by a definite form of action, but the belief that any form of social constraint of others or any violent action is in itself wrong, and that violence such as War must be *passively* resisted because to use violence to end violence would be logically self-contradictory. I oppose pacifism in this sense to the Communist belief that the only way to secure peace is by a revolutionary change in the social system, and that ruling classes resist revolution violently and must therefore be overthrown by force.

But modern war is also distinctively bourgeois. Struggles such as the last war arise from the unequal Imperialist development of the bourgeois powers. and earlier wars of bourgeois culture were also fought for aims characteristic of bourgeois economy or, like the wars of the infant Dutch republic, represented the struggles of the growing bourgeois class against feudal forces. In its last stage of Fascism, when capitalism, throwing off the democratic forms which no longer serve its purpose, rules with open violence, bourgeois culture is also seen as aggressively militant. Are we Marxists then simply using labels indiscriminately when we class as characteristically bourgeois, both militancy *and* pacifism, meekness *and* violence ?

No, we are not doing so, if we can show that we call bourgeois not all war and not all pacifism but only certain types of violence, and only certain types of non-violence ; and if, further, we can show how the one fundamental bourgeois position generates both these apparently opposed viewpoints. We did the same thing when we showed that two philosophies which are apparently completely opposed—mechanical materialism and idealism—were both characteristically bourgeois, and both generated by the one bourgeois assumption.

Bourgeois pacifism is distinctive and should not be confused, for example, with Eastern pacifism, any more than modern European warfare should be confused with feudal warfare. It is not merely that the social manifestations of it are different—this would necessarily arise from the different social organs of the two cultures. But the content also is different. Anyone who supposes that bourgeois pacifism will, for example, take the form of a University Anti-War Group lying down on the rails in front of a departing troop train like an Indian pacifist group, is to be ignorant of the nature of bourgeois pacifism and of whence it took its colour. The historic example of bourgeois pacifism is not Gandhi but Fox. The Society of Friends expresses the spirit of bourgeois pacifism. It is individual resistance.

To understand how bourgeois pacifism arises, we must understand how bourgeois violence arises. It arises, just as does feudal or despotic violence, from the characteristic economy of the system. As was first explained by Marx, the characteristics of bourgeois economy are that the bourgeois, held down and crippled productively by the feudal system, comes to see freedom and productive growth in lack of social organisation, in every man's administering his own affairs for his own benefit to the best of his ability and desire, and this is expressed in the absolute character of bourgeois property together with its complete alienability. His struggle to achieve this right did secure his greater freedom and productive power as compared with his position in the feudal system. The circumstances of the struggle and its outcome gave rise to the bourgeois dream—freedom as the absolute elimination of social relations.

But such a programme, if carried into effect, would mean the end of society and the break-down of economic production. Each man would struggle for himself, and if he saw another man with something he wanted, he would seize it, for by assumption no such social relations as co-operation exist. The saving and foresight which makes economic production possible would cease to exist. Man would become a brute.

But in fact the bourgeois had no desire for such a world. He lived by merchandising and banking, by *capital* as opposed to the land which was the basis of feudal exploitation. Therefore he meant by the ' absence of social restraints ', the absence of any restraint on his ownership, alienation, or acquisition at will of the capital by which he lived. Private property is a social ' restraint ', for others not owning it are ' restrained ' from helping themselves to it by force or cunning, as they could in a ' state of nature '; but the bourgeois never included the ownership of capital as one of the social restraints that should be abolished, for the simple reason that it was not to him a restraint at all. It never therefore entered his head to regard it as such, and he saw nothing inconsistent in calling for the abolition of privilege, monopoly, and so forth, while hanging on to his capital.

Moreover, he had a cogent argument which, when he became more self-conscious, he could use. A social restraint is a social relation, that is, a relation between men. The relation between master and slave is a social relation and therefore a restraint on the liberty of one man by the other. In the same way the relation between lord and serf is a relation between men and a restraint on human liberty; but the relation between a man and his property is a relation between man and a thing, and is therefore no restraint on the liberty of other men.

This argument was of course fallacious, for there can be no universal relations of this kind as the fabric of society, there can only be relations between men disguised as relations between things. The bourgeois defence of private property only applies if I go out into the woods and pick up a stick to walk with, or fashion an ornamental object for my adornment; it applies to the possession of socially unimportant trifles or things for immediate consumption. As soon as bourgeois possession extends to the capital of the community, consisting of the products of the community set aside to produce goods in the future (in early bourgeois civilisation, grain, clothes, seed and raw materials to supply the labourers of to-morrow, and in addition machinery and plant for the same purpose to-day), this relation to a thing becomes a relation among men, for it is now the labour of the community which the bourgeois controls. The bourgeois right of private property leads to this, that on the one hand the world and all that society has created in it belongs to the bourgeois, and on the other hand stands the naked labourer, who is forced by the needs of his body to sell his labour-power to the bourgeois in order to feed himself and his master. The bourgeois will only buy his labour-power, if he makes a profit from it. This social relation is only made possible by—it *depends on*—the bourgeois ownership of capital. Thus, just as in slave-owning or serf-owning civilisation there is a relation between men which is a relation between a dominating and a dominated class, or between exploiters and exploited ; so there is in bourgeois culture, but whereas in earlier civilisations this relation between men is conscious and clear, in bourgeois culture it is disguised as a system free from obligatory dominating relations between men and containing only innocent relations between men and a thing.

Therefore, in throwing off all social restraint, the bourgeois seemed to himself justified in retaining this one restraint of private property, for it did not seem to him a restraint at all, but an inalienable right of man, the fundamental natural right. Unfortunately for this theory, there are no natural rights, only situations found in nature, and private property protected for one man by others is not one of them. Bourgeois private property could only be protected by coercion—the *have-nots* had to be coerced by the *haves* after all, just as in feudal society. Thus a dominating relation as violent as in slave-owning civilisations came into being, expressed in the police, the laws, the standing army, and the legal apparatus of the bourgeois State. The whole bourgeois State revolves round the coercive protection of private property, alienable and acquirable by trading for private profit, and regarded as a natural right, but a right which, strangely enough, can only be protected by coercion, because it involves of its essence a right to dispose of and extract profit from the labour-power of others, and so administer their lives.

Thus, after all, the bourgeois dream of liberty cannot be realised. Social restraints must come into being to protect this one thing that makes him a bourgeois. This ' freedom ' to own private property seems to him inexplicably to involve more and more social restraints, laws, tariffs, and factory acts ; and this ' society ' in which only relations to a thing are permitted becomes more and more a society in which relations between men are elaborate and cruel. The more he aims for bourgeois freedom, the more he gets bourgeois restraint, for bourgeois freedom is an illusion.

Thus, just as much as in slave-owning society, bourgeois society turns out to be a society built on violent coercion of men by men, the more violent in that while the master must feed and protect his slave, whether he works or not, the bourgeois employer owns no obligation to the free labourer, not even to find him work. The whole bourgeois dream explodes in practice, and the bourgeois state becomes a theatre of the violent and coercive subjection of man to man for the purposes of economic production.

For the purposes of economic production. Unlike the violence of the footpad, the violence of the bourgeois though similar in motive plays a social rôle. It is the relation whereby social production is secured in bourgeois society, just as the master-to-slave relation secures production in a slave-owning civilisation. It is for its epoch the best method of securing production, and it is better to be a slave than a beast of the jungle, better to be an exploited labourer than a slave, not because the bourgeois employer is ' nicer ' than the slave-owner (he is often a good deal crueller), but because the wealth of society as a whole is more with the former relation than the latter.

But no system of relations is static, it develops and changes. Slave-owning relations develop into Empires and then reveal their internal contradictions. They collapse. The story of the collapse of the Roman Empire is the story of the constant decline of the taxable wealth of the Empire between Augustus and Justinian as a result of increasing exploitation until, a poverty-stricken shell, it crumbled before the assaults of the barbarian, up till then easily repelled. In the same way, feudal civilisation, exhausted in England by the anarchy of the Wars of the Roses, collapsed. But not this time, before an external enemy ; it fell before an internal enemy, the rising bourgeois class.

Bourgeois relations, too, developed. In the famous bourgeois booms and slumps, they show the potential decay of the system. This decay was retarded by Imperialism, that is, by forcibly imposing on other countries the ' natural rights ' of the bourgeois. In these backward countries the bourgeois right to trade profitably and to alienate and acquire any property was forcibly imposed. Here too the bourgeois, out of his dominating relation to a thing, secretly imposed his dominating relation over men, which can yet be disguised as democracy, for does not democracy declare that all men are equal and none may enslave the other ? Does it not exclude all relations of domination—

despotism, slave-owning, feudal privilege—except the 'innocent' domination of capitalist over 'free' labourer?

But in this imperialising, a new situation arose—*external* war instead of *internal* violence and coercion. For now, in exploiting backward countries, or, it was called, 'civilising' them, one bourgeois State found itself competing with another, just as inside the State bourgeois competes with bourgeois.

But inside the State bourgeois competes with bourgeois peacefully, because it is the law—and this law was established for their own protection against the exploited. The laws forbidding one bourgeois to seize another's property by force arose as the result of the need to prevent the have-nots seizing property by force. It is an internal law, the law of the coercive State. If it had not been necessary for the existence of the whole bourgeois class for them to be protected against the seizing of their property by the exploited, the law against the forcible seizure of private property, coercively enforced and taught to the exploited as a 'necessary' law of society, would never have come into existence. For the individualistic, competitive nature of bourgeois trade (each 'getting the better' of the other) is such that no bourgeois sees anything wrong in impoverishing another bourgeois. If he is 'bust' or 'hammered'—well, it's the luck of the game. But all unite as a class against the exploited, for the existence of the class depends on this. If it is a case of a battle royal *inside* the bourgeois class, each bourgeois believes by nature and education that, given an equal chance, he will get the better of the other. This eternal optimism of the bourgeois is seen in the historic bourgeois appeals for 'fair-play', 'fair field and no favour', and all the other allied bourgeois slogans which express the ethics of the 'sporting' English gentleman.

It is quite different when the bourgeois States, through their coercive organisations, find themselves competing in the world arena for the backward lands. There is now no numerous exploited class menacing the existence of the class of bourgeois States *as a whole. Inside* the coercive State, if it came to a 'show-down', with street-fighting, bare hands, and man against man—the exploited would win. But in the Imperialistic arena the bourgeois States appear as highly developed organisms, for, thanks to the unification of the coercive State, they now dispose of all the resources of an advanced society, including the services, in the army, of the exploited class itself. The backward nations still play inside the world arena the rôle of the exploited class inside the State, but they are not a danger to the class of bourgeois States as a whole, as is the exploited class to the class of bourgeois as a whole inside the State. They are just inanimate things, almost defenceless, so much dead undeveloped territory.

There is then no world danger threatening the class of bourgeois States as a whole, as, in a State, revolution threatens the class of bourgeois as a whole. There is only individual competition among bourgeois States, and, as we have seen, the bourgeois never minds this.

All he asks for is 'fair field and no favour' and he is certain that he will come out on top. He feels no need for a law to restrain competition among bourgeois. Hence the sovereign bourgeois State comes into being and battles bloodily with other bourgeois States for the booty of the backward territory. This is the age of Imperialism, culminating in the Great War.

Needless to say, the bourgeois finds the bourgeois dream—'a fair field and no favour'—when realised for the first time, far bloodier and more violent than he dreamed. War presently comes to seem to him 'unfair competition'. Like a price-cutting war, it alarms him and he feels someone from outside ought to stop it. He calls for aid ; but there is no one 'outside'. For to whom, on heaven or earth, can he call, as a member of the class of independent *sovereign* States ?

Still he has a dream. If the class of bourgeois in *one* country can have a State and police force enforcing order and non-violent competition, why not a State of States, a world-State, in which world peace is enforced ?

This bourgeois hope perpetually recurs in the chaos of war, and the League of Nations is one form of it. But the one factor which secures internal law in the bourgeois State—the existence of a dangerous exploited class—does not exist in the *world* arena. No danger confronts the class of bourgeois States *as a whole*, and thus they can never unite to accept a coercive regulating law superior to their own wills. The danger only exists as among themselves and each, like a good bourgeois, believes that, by appropriate 'combination', treaty-making, and manœuvring, he can best the others. The bourgeois dream of a peaceful Imperialism is unrealisable for want of a danger common to all bourgeois States to unite them. After a bitter experience of the unpleasantness of war, as after a bitter experience of the unpleasantness of price-cutting, they can unite in a voluntary cartel, the League of Nations, but like a cartel it lacks the cohesion and coercive power of the bourgeois State and therefore lacks also its efficiency in mediating between bourgeois. It is like a price agreement to which all voluntarily adhere for their own individual benefit. Since, in bourgeois production in general, and Imperialist exploitation in particular, an agreement cannot work always for the good of all, it is only a matter of time before the cartel is denounced by some and we see the *have-not* bourgeois States (Germany and Italy) are outside the cartel, and arrayed against the *haves* (France and England), while that bourgeois State (America) whose interests do not lie in the same sphere of Imperialist exploitation, has never joined the cartel. Thus in spite of the bitterest lessons possible to a nation, proving the inefficiency of war as a palliative of slump, it is not possible for States whose forms coercively express bourgeois interests to acknowledge a superior co-ordinating force, which would produce in the international sphere legal machinery like that securing internal order in the State, for this internal machinery is directed against the dangerous exploited class, and in the international sphere there is no dangerous exploited class. Thus the peaceful World

Federation of States, the League, becomes part of the bourgeois illusion, and the nations arm themselves still more heavily.

Could not Russia, as a proletarian State, furnish the equivalent in the international sphere of the exploited class, and force the independent bourgeois States to unite and crush her? This was the Trotsky nightmare, from which it followed that Socialism could not be established anywhere without a world revolution. But this theory overlooked the fact that Soviet Russia is not an exploited State. An exploited class, in a bourgeois State, is a class held up to ransom by the bourgeois, who hold the means of production in their hands. It is a case of: 'Work for us or die.' Such a situation can only be maintained by moral and physical coercion and therefore bourgeois 'rights' have to be maintained in this way perpetually; otherwise men would not naturally tolerate a situation where their very means of livelihood were in another's hands and could be only secured if they generated profit for that other. But in Russia this class has expropriated their expropriators. It is not a case of working for other bourgeois States or dying; the Russian workers are their own masters. Moreover, unlike other bourgeois States, there are no internal contradictions in their economy (accumulation of capital) forcing them to seek new fields of exploitation.

Russia appears, therefore, in the world arena, to the bourgeois States, not as an exploited class inherently dangerous but as an ordinary internally ordered coercive

State—' one of themselves '. She competes with them in open world markets but, for reasons that do not concern them, does not seek backward countries on which to impose Imperialist exploitation. She can therefore join their cartel. In this cartel her duty is to join the bourgeois game—playing one alliance off against another—not to gain Imperialistic advantage but in order to secure peace for herself and for the unfortunate proletariat of the bourgeois States.

It is true that Russia is a danger to all bourgeois States in that her success is an inspiration to a proletarian revolution in every State. But the world proletarian revolution means the end of bourgeois economy, and this, to the bourgeois, is at first simply ludicrous. On the one hand he tells himself that Bolshevism is only a ' passing phase ', and, on the other hand, that in modern Soviet Russia there is simply ' planned capitalism '. Moreover, the proletarian revolution will not come from Russia, it will come from inside, and it would therefore be pointless to attempt to stop, say, the British proletariat from rising by attacking Russia. On the contrary, such a move would hasten the very event that is dreaded. Thus, although the bourgeois States denounce Russia, they cannot be united in one common attack on her, but instead are ready to enter into pacts with her, to use her against each other.

That is not to say Russia is not in danger. On the contrary, all bourgeois States are in danger from each other in so far as they represent possible fields of Imperialistic exploitation. In this respect Russia is in as much danger from Germany as Britain from Germany. It is therefore necessary for her to arm herself as heavily as her bourgeois neighbours and try to strengthen herself by pacts, the international equivalent of cartels and trade agreements.

Only when the bourgeois begins to see the inevitability of Communism does he begin to regard Russia as a greater danger than any other bourgeois State. But this realisation is just what causes the capitalist class to resort to Fascism and therefore the Fascist States constitute the main danger to Russia to-day.

. . . . .

This, then, is the analysis of bourgeois violence. It is not like something that descends from heaven for a time to madden the human race. It is implicit in the bourgeois illusion.

The whole bourgeois economy is built on the violent domination of men by men through the private possession of social capital. It is always there, waiting ready at any moment to flame out in a Peterloo or an Amritzar within the bourgeois State, or a Boer War or Great War outside it.

As long as the bourgeois economy remains a positive constructive force, that violence is hidden. Society does not contain a powerful internal pressure until productive forces have outgrown the system of productive relations. Until this revolutionary pressure develops, it is therefore for coercion to show itself bloodily or on a wide scale.

But when bourgeois economy is riven by its own

contradictions, when private profit is seen to be public harm, when poverty and unemployment grow in the midst of the means of plenty, bourgeois violence becomes more open. These contradictions drive the bourgeois States to Imperialistic wars, in which violence reigns without a qualifying factor. Internally violence instead of 'reason' alone suffices to maintain the bourgeois system. Since the capitalistic system is openly proving its inefficiency, people are no longer content with a form of government, parliamentary democracy, in which economic production is run by the bourgeois class, leaving the people as a whole only the power to settle, within narrow limits, through Parliament, the apportionment of a merely administrative budget. They see this to be a sham, and see no reason to tolerate the sham. There is a growing demand for socialism, and the capitalist class where this grows pressing, resort to open violence. They use the revolt against ineffectual democracy to establish a dictatorship, and this dictatorship, which seizes power with the cry 'Down with Capitalism', in fact establishes capitalism still more violently, as in Fascist Italy and Germany. The brutal oppression and cynical violence of Fascism is the summit of bourgeois decline. The violence at the heart of the bourgeois illusion emerges inside as well as outside the State.

The justification of bourgeois violence is an important part of bourgeois ethics. The coercive control of social labour by a limited class is justified as a relation to a thing. Even as late as Hegel, this justification is given quite naïvely and simply. Just as I go out and break off a stick of wood from the primitive jungle and convert it to my purpose, so the bourgeois is supposed to convert the thing 'capital' to his use. Domination over men is wicked; domination over things is legitimate.

The nature of bourgeois economy made it possible for Hegel to believe this seriously. But when the true nature of bourgeois economy had been analysed by Marx, as a dominating relation over men through ownership of the means of social labour and individual livelihood, how could this naïve bourgeois attitude persist? Only by vilifying Marx, by always attacking him violently without explaining his views, and by continuing to teach, preach and practise the old bourgeois theory. It was then that the bourgeois illusion became the bourgeois lie, a conscious deception festering at the heart of bourgeois culture.

Bourgeois ethics include the more difficult task of justification of the violence of bourgeois war. The Christian-bourgeois ethic has been equal even to this. Consonant to the bourgeois illusion, all interference with the liberty of another is wicked and immoral. If one is attacked in one's liberty, one is therefore compelled to defend outraged morality and attack in turn. All bourgeois wars are therefore justified by both parties as wars of defence. Bourgeois liberty includes the right to exercise all bourgeois occupations—alienating, trading, and acquiring for profit—and since these involve establishing dominating relations over others, it is not surprising that the bourgeois often finds himself attacked in his liberty. It is impossible for the bourgeois to exercise his full liberty without infringing the liberty of another. It is impossible therefore to be thoroughly bourgeois and not give occasion for 'just' wars.

Meanwhile bourgeois discomforts generate an opposition to bourgeois violence. At each stage of bourgeois development men could be found who were impregnated with the bourgeois illusion, that man is free and happy only when without social restraints, and who yet found in bourgeois economy multiplying coercions and restraints. We saw why these exist; the bourgeois economy requires coercion and restraint for its very life. The big bourgeois dominates the *petit bourgeois*, just as both dominate the proletariat. But these early bourgeois rebels could not see this. They demanded a return to the bourgeois dream—'equal rights for all', 'freedom from social restraints', the 'natural rights' of men. They thought that this would free them from the big bourgeoisie, and give them equal competition once again.

Thus originated the cleavage between conservatives and liberals, between the big bourgeois in possession and the little bourgeois wishing to be in possession. The one sees that his position depends on maintaining things as they are; the other sees his as depending on more bourgeois freedom, more votes for all, more freedom for private property to be alienated, acquired, and owned, more free competition, less privilege.

The liberal is the active force. But so far from being

revolutionary, as he thinks, he is evolutionary. In striving for bourgeois freedom and fair competition he produces by this very action an increase in the social restraints he hates. He builds up the big bourgeoisie in trying to support the little, although he may make himself a big bourgeois in the process. He increases unfairness by trying to secure fairness. Free trade gives birth to tariffs, Imperialism and monopoly, because it is hastening the development of bourgeois economy, and these things are the necessary end of bourgeois development. He calls into being the things he loathes because, as long as he is in the grip of the bourgeois illusion that freedom consists in absence of social planning, he must put himself, by loosening social ties, more powerfully in the grip of coercive social forces.

This 'revolutionary' liberal, this hater of coercion and violence, this lover of free competition, this friend of liberty and human rights, is therefore the very man damned by history not merely to be powerless to stop these things, but to be forced by his own efforts to produce coercion and violence and unfair competition and slavery. He does not merely refrain from opposing bourgeois violence, he generates it, by helping on the development of bourgeois economy.

To-day, as the bourgeois pacifist, he helps to generate the violence, war, and Fascist and Imperialist brutality he hates. In so far as he is a genuine pacifist and not merely a completely muddled man hesitating between the paths of revolution and non-co-operation, his thesis is this, 'I hate violence and war and social oppression, and all these things are due to social relations. I must therefore abstain from social relations. Belligerent and revolutionary alike are hateful to me.'

But to abstain from social relations, is to abstain from life. As long as he draws or earns an income, he participates in bourgeois economy, and upholds the violence which sustains it. He is in sleeping partnership with the big bourgeoisie, and that is the essence of bourgeois economy. If two other countries are at war, he is powerless to intervene and stop them, for that means social co-operation—social co-operation issuing in coercion, like a man separating quarrelling friends, and that action is by his definition barred to him. If the big bourgeoisie of his own country decide to go to war and mobilise the coercive forces, physical and moral, of the State, he can do nothing real, for the only real answer is co-operation with the proletariat to resist the coercive action of the big bourgeoisie and oust them from power. If Fascism develops, he cannot suppress it in the bud before it has built up an army to intimidate the proletariat, for he believes in 'free speech'. He can only watch the workers being bludgeoned and beheaded by the forces he allowed to develop.

His position rests firmly on the bourgeois fallacy. He thinks that man as an individual has power. He does not see that even in the unlikely event of everyone's taking his viewpoint and saying, 'I will passively resist,' his purpose will still not be achieved. For men cannot in fact cease to co-operate, because society's work must be carried on—grain must be reaped, clothes spun, electricity generated or man will perish from the earth. Only his position as a member of a parasitic class could have given him any other illusion. A worker sees that his very life depends on economic co-operation and that this co-operation of itself imposes social relations which in bourgeois economy must be bourgeois, that is, must in greater or less measure give into the hands of the big bourgeoisie the violent issues of life and death. Passive resistance is not a real programme, but an apology for supporting the old programme. A man either participates in bourgeois economy, or he revolts and tries to establish another economy. Another apparent road is to break up society and return to the jungle, the solution of *anarchy*. But that is no solution at all. The only real alternative to bourgeois economy is proletarian economy, i.e. socialism, and therefore one either participates in bourgeois economy or is a proletarian revolutionary. The fact that one participates passively in bourgeois economy, that one does not oneself wield the bludgeon or fire the cannon, so far from being a defence really make one's position more disgusting, just as a fence is more unpleasant than a burglar, and a pimp than a prostitute. One lets others do the dirty work, and merely participates in the benefit. The bourgeois pacifist occupies perhaps the most ignoble place of a man in any civilisation. He is the Christian Protestant whose ethics have been made ridiculous by the development of the culture that evolved them ; but this does not prevent his deriving complacency from observing them. He sits on the head of the worker and, while the big bourgeois kicks him, advises him to lie quiet. When (as did some pacifists during the general strike) he 'maintains essential services' during the 'violent' struggles of the proletariat for freedom, he becomes a portent.

Pacifism, for all its specious moral aspect, is, like Protestant Christianity, the creed of ultra-individualism and selfishness, just as Roman Catholicism is the creed of monopoly and privileged domination. This selfishness is seen in all the defences the bourgeois pacifist makes of his creed.

The first defence is that it is wrong. It is a 'sin' to slay or resort to violence. Christ forbids it. The pacifist who resorts to violence imbrues his soul with heinous guilt. In this conception nothing appears as important but the pacifist's own soul. It is this precious soul of his that he is worrying about, like the good bourgeoise about her honour which is such an important social asset. Society can go to the devil if his soul is intact. So imbued is he with bourgeois notions of sin, that it never occurs to him that a preoccupation with one's own soul and one's own salvation is selfish. It may be that a man is right to save his own skin before all; that the pacifist above all must prevent the contamination of his precious soul by the mortal sin of violence. But what is this but the translation into spiritual terms of the good old bourgeois rule of *laissez-faire* and bourgeoisdom—May the devil take the hindmost? It is a spiritual *laissez-faire*. It is a belief that the interests of society—*God's* purpose—are best served by not performing any action, however beneficial to others, if it would imperil one's own 'soul'. This is crystallised in the maxim, 'One may not do ill that good may come of it.'

Primitives have a more social conception of sin. Sin is reprehensible because it involves the whole tribe in danger. The sinner flees from the tribe because he has involved it in evil, not in order to save himself; he is damned by his sin. Going into the desert, he slays himself or is slain, thus lifting from the tribe, after it has performed appropriate purifications, the evil in which he has involved it. Both conceptions are bound in error, but this savage conception is nobler and more altruistic than the bourgeois conception in which each man is responsible solely for his own sins, and purifies them by a private resort to the blood of Christ. The pacifist has remembered the saying of Cain: 'Am I my brother's keeper?'

This tribal conception of salvation was partly retained in feudal society by the Church, which kept clearly in mind the unity of the Church Militant, the Church Suffering, and the Church Triumphant, each of which, by its prayers, could communicate with or help the others. The feudal Christian prayed for the Holy Souls suffering in Purgatory, expected those living to pray for him when dead, and continually called on the departed members of the tribe, the Triumphant Souls of the Saints in heaven, to help him, to such an extent that, in this strong social grouping, God was almost forgotten. The social unity alone emerges, and individual sin becomes pardoned by the mere act of socialisation, in the confessional.

Thus Catholicism symbolised the social nature of feudalism ; the ' tribe ' was all Christendom. Its typical act was the Crusade, the violent assault of Christendom on paganism.

Protestantism, the religion of the bourgeoisie, necessarily revolted against tribal Catholicism. As a religion, it ' reformed ' all the social elements in Catholicism. It became Catholicism minus the social elements and plus individualism. Authority was abandoned ; the priest, the repository of the magic and conscience of the tribe was shorn of his power ; the prayers for the dead and to the saints were unindividualistic, therefore purgatory did not exist and the saints were helpless. Each man was to be his own judge, bear his own sin, and work out his own salvation. The notion of individual guilt, as in Bunyan and the Puritans, reached a pitch it had never achieved in Catholic countries. Hence too the new phenomena of ' conversion ', in which this intolerable self-induced burden of guilt is thrown into the bosom of Christ. For man cannot in fact live alone. This conversion was evidence of it ; that the individualism of bourgeoisdom is only a façade, and that at the very moment he proclaims it, the individual needs some fictitious entity or Divine Scapegoat on whom he can fling, in a final act of selfishness, the responsibility he never completely bore.

Thus Pacifism, as a method of avoiding the moral guilt of violence, is selfish. The pacifist claims, as a primary duty, the right of saving his *own* skin. We are not concerned with whether it is ethically right for man to consider himself first. To the bourgeois philosophy, properly expressed, it is so. To another system of social relations it cannot be right. To a third—communism, it is neither right nor wrong, it is impossible, for all individual actions affect others in society. This fact makes the bourgeois inconsistent, and at one moment want to give his life for others and at the next to sacrifice their lives to preserve his soul.

Some pacifists, however, make a different defence. They are not concerned with their own souls. They are only thinking of others. Pacifism is the only way to stop violence and oppression. Violence breeds violence; oppression breeds oppression. How far is this argument well grounded, and not merely a rationalisation of the bourgeois illusion?

No pacifist has yet explained the causal chain by which non-resistance ends violence. It is true that it does so in this obvious way, that if no resistance is made to violent commands, no violence is necessary to enforce them. Thus if A does everything B asks him, it will not be necessary for B to use violence. But a dominating relation of this kind is in essence violent, although violence is not overtly shown. Subjection is subjection, and rapacity rapacity, even if the weakness of the victim, or the fear inspired by the victor, makes the process non-forcible. Non-resistance will not prevent it, any more than the lack of claws on the part of prey prevents carnivores battening on them. On the contrary, the carnivore selects as his victim animals of the kind. The remedy is the elimination of carnivores, that is, the extinction of classes that live by preying on others.

Another assumption is that man, being what he is, the sight of his defenceless victims will arouse his pity. Now this assumption is not in itself ridiculous, but it needs examination. Is it a historical fact that the defencelessness of his victims has ever aroused man's pity? History records millions of opposite cases, of Tamburlane and his atrocities, Attila and his Huns (checked only by violence), Mohammedan incursions, primitive slayings, the Danes and their monastic massacres. Can anyone in good faith advance the proposition that non-resistance defeats violence? How could slave-owning states exist, if peaceful submission touched the hearts of the conquerors? How could man bear to slaughter perpetually the dumb unresisting races of sheep, swine, and oxen?

Moreover, the argument makes the usual bourgeois error of eternalising its categories, the belief that there is a kind of abstract Robinson Crusoe man of whose actions definite predictions can be made. But how can one seriously subsume under one category Tamburlane, Socrates, a Chinese mandarin, a modern Londoner, an Aztec priest, a Paleolithic hunter, and a Roman galley-slave? There is no abstract man, but men in different networks of social relations, with similar heredities but moulded into different proclivities by education and the constant pressure of social being.

To-day, it is man in bourgeois social relations with

whom we are concerned. Of what effect would it be if we no longer resisted violence, if England, for example, at the beginning of the Great War, had passively permitted Germany to occupy Belgium, and accept without resistance all that Germany wished to do?

There is this much truth in the pacifist argument: that a country in a state of bourgeois social relations cannot act like a nomad horde. Bourgeoisdom has discovered that Tamburlane exploitation does not pay so well as bourgeois exploitation. It is of no use to a bourgeois to sweep over a country, to lift all the wine and fair women and gold thereof and sweep out again. The fair women grow old and ugly, the wine is drunk, and the gold avails for nothing but ornaments. That would be Dead Sea fruit in the mouth of bourgeois culture, which lives on an endless diet of profit and a perpetual domination.

Bourgeois culture has discovered that what pays is bourgeois violence. This is more subtle and less overt than Tamburlane violence. Roman violence, which consisted in bringing home not only fair women and gold, but slaves also, and making them work in the household, farms, and mines, occupied a mid-position. Bourgeois culture has discovered that those social relations are most profitable to the bourgeois which do not include rapine and personal slavery, but on the contrary forbid it. Therefore the bourgeois, wherever he has conquered non-bourgeois territory, such as Australia, America, Africa, or India, has imposed bourgeois, not Tamburlane, social relations. In the name of liberty, self-determination, and democracy, or sometimes without these names, they enforce the bourgeois essence, private property, and the ownership of the means of production for profit, and its necessary prerequisite, the free labourer forced to dispose of his labour, for a wage, in the market. This priceless bourgeois discovery has produced material wealth beyond the dreams of a Tamburlane or a Crœsus.

Consequently England need have no fear that a victorious Germany would have raped all Englishwomen and beheaded all Englishmen and transported the Elgin marbles to Berlin. Bourgeois States do not do such things. It would have confined itself to taking England's Imperial possessions and completing the profitable task of converting them to full bourgeois social relations. It would also have attempted to cripple England as a trade competitor by a heavy indemnity. In other words, resist or not, it would, if victorious, have done to England what victorious England did to Germany.

Thus, even if the pacifist dream was realised, bourgeois violence would go on. But in fact it would not be realised. How could a bourgeois coercive State submit to having its source of profits violently taken away by another bourgeois State, and not use all the sources of violence at its disposal to stop it? Would it not rather disrupt the whole internal fabric of its State than permit such a thing? Is bourgeoisdom not now disrupting violently the whole fabric of society, rather than forgo its private profits and give up the system of economy on which it is based? Fascism and

Nazism, bloodily treading the road to bankruptcy, are evidence of this. Bourgeois economy, because it is unplanned, will cut its own throat rather than reform, and pacifism is only the expression of this last-ditch stand of bourgeois culture, which will at the best rather do nothing than do the thing that will end the social relations on which it is based.

Have we the courage to realise forcibly our views ? What guarantee have we of their truth ? The only real guarantee *is* action. We have the courage to enforce our beliefs upon physical matter, to build up the material substratum of society in houses, roads, bridges, and ships, despite the risk to human life, because our theories, generated by action, are tested in action. Let the bridge fall, the ship sink, the house collapse if we are wrong. We have investigated the causality of nature ; let it be proved upon ourselves if we are wrong.

Exactly the same applies to social relations. Bridges have collapsed before now, cultures have mouldered in decay, vast civilisations have foundered, but they did not decay uselessly. From each mistake we have learned something, and the Tamburlane society, the slave-owning society, the feudal society, proved upon the test of action have failed. Yet it has only been partial failure ; with each we learned a little more, just as the most recent bridge embodies lessons learned from the collapse of the first. Always the lesson was the same, it was the violence, the dominating relation between master and slave, lord and serf, bourgeois and proletarian, which was the weakness in the bridge.

But the pacifist, like all bourgeois theoreticians, is obsessed with the lazy lust of the absolute. 'Give me,' they all cry, 'absolute truth, absolute justice, some rule-of-thumb standard by which I can evade the strenuous task of finding the features of reality by intimate contact with it in action. Give me some logical talisman, some philosopher's stone, by which I can test all acts in theory and say, this is right. Give me some principle such as, *Violence is wrong*, so that I can simply refrain from all violent action and know that I am right.' But the only absolute they find is the standard of bourgeois economy. 'Abstain from social action.' Standards are made, not found.

Man cannot live without acting. Even to cease to act, to let things go their own way, is a form of acting, as when I drop a stone that perhaps starts an avalanche. And since man is always acting, he is always exerting force, always altering or maintaining the position of things, always revolutionary or conservative. Existence is the exercise of force on the physical environment and on other men. The web of physical and social relations that binds men into one universe ensures that nothing we do is without its effect on others, whether we vote or cease to vote, whether we help the police or let them go their way, whether we let two combatants fight or separate them forcibly or assist one against the other, whether we let a man starve to death or move heaven and earth to assist him. Man can never rest on the absolute; all acts involve consequences, and it is man's task to find out these consequences, and act accordingly. He can never choose between action and inaction, he can only choose between life and death. He can never absolve himself with the ancient plea, 'My intentions were good', or 'I meant it for the best', or 'I have broken no commandment'. Even savages have a more vital conception than this, with whom an act is judged by its consequences, even as a bridge is judged by its stability. Therefore it is man's task to find out the consequences of acts : which means discovering the laws of social relations, the impulses, causes and effects of history.

Thus it is beside the point to ask the pacifist whether he would have defended Greece from the Persian or his sister from a would-be ravisher. Modern society imposes a different and more concrete issue. Under which banner of violence will he impose himself? The violence of bourgeois relations, or the violence not only to resist them but to end them? Bourgeois social relations are revealing, more and more insistently, the violence of exploitation and dispossession on which they are founded ; more and more they harrow man with brutality and oppression. By abstaining from action the pacifist enrolls himself under this banner, the banner of things as they are and getting worse, the banner of the increasing violence and coercion exerted by the *haves* on the *have-nots*. He calls increasingly into being the violences of poverty, deprivation, artificial slumps, artistic and scientific decay, fascism, and war.

Or he can enroll himself under the revolutionary banner, of things as they will be. In doing so he accepts the stern necessity that he who is to replace a truth or an institution or a system of social relations, must substitute a better, that he who is to pull down a bridge, however inefficient, must put instead a better bridge. Bourgeois social relations were better perhaps than slave-owning, what can the revolutionary find better than them? And, having found them, how is he to bring them about? For one must not only plan the bridge, one must see how it is to be built, by violence, by force, by blasting the living rock and tugging and sweating at the stones that make it.

Thus, for the negativism of pacifism, which shores up the decaying world and tolerates man's increasing misery, the revolutionary must substitute the positivism of communism. He must forge a new economy adequate to take over bourgeois social relations and purge them of the coercive violence at their heart. But this violence grew from a class relation, the domination of an exploited by an exploiting class. To end this violence means building the classless State. Hating the violence of the bourgeois State, either in peace or war, the revolutionary must produce a society which needs neither violence in peace nor in war. Since it is material reality with which he is dealing, he must see the only path by which bourgeois social relations of violence can be turned into peaceful communist social relations. It is the path of revolution and the dictatorship of the proletariat, followed by the withering away of the State. If he does not clearly see—as an architect sees the building of foundations, and the transportation of material—this mode of transformation of bourgeois violence into communist peace, his socialism remains an empty dream, he is still at heart a pacifist, a partisan of things as they are, you will still find him in fact, for all his theoretical protestations, enrolled beneath the banner of bourgeois violence, strike-breaking or giving Fascism 'free speech'.

To expropriate the expropriators, to oppose their coercion by that of the workers, to destroy all the instruments of class coercion and exploitation crystallised in the bourgeois State, is the first task. Who can lead the struggle but the exploited, and not only all the exploited but those whose very exploitation has organised them, massed them together, and made them co-operate socially, the proletariat. Since a dispossessed class will fight to the last ditch, while there is hope, how can the transition be affected other than violently, substituting the dictatorship of the proletariat and its necessary forms for the former dictatorship of the bourgeoisie and its characteristic forms?

But whereas the dictatorship of the bourgeois minority perpetuated itself, because the dispossessed class was also the exploited class, the dictatorship of the proletarian majority does not perpetuate itself, for it does not exploit the dispossessed class, but is itself both owner and worker of the means of production. Thus, as the dispossessed class disappears, the dictatorship of the proletariat in all its forms withers away. The pacifist's dream is realised. Violence departs from the world of men. Man at last becomes free.

VI

LOVE

A STUDY IN CHANGING VALUES

THE natural human failing is to suppose nothing changes, that ideas are eternal, and that what is denoted by a word is as changeless and invariant as the word. Wisdom consists chiefly in learning that those vague gestures towards parts of reality, gestures we call concepts, not only cannot describe the thing indicated, but cannot even point to the same thing, only to something *divers et ondoyant* flashing to our interested eyes in the process of becoming. The dog subsumes all small running things under the concept 'prey'. He does not utter it as a word, but still shows the unvarying nature of his concept by a stereotyped action of pursuit. We can see his foolishness, for we have divided 'prey' into rabbits, rats, and cats, even perhaps into individual cats with different habits. But at a higher level of reference we make the same kind of mistake.

We tend to think, for example, that love is something definite and quite clear. If we are romantic poets, novelists or film-goers, we are in danger of picturing it as a kind of Paradisial pit into which we fall. There is no doubt about it, either we are over the edge and deep in, or safe outside it. To the instinct psychologist love is an innate response, i.e. a clearly defined behaviour pattern set off by certain stimuli, just as an automatic model is set going by putting a penny in the slot. To the psychoanalyst, love is a quantity of psychic energy, called libido, as limited and homogenous as a pound of suet, which is parcelled by repressions and inhibition into various channels, returns on itself, is transferred, cathexed and displaced, but is still visualised as the same consistent suet.

But 'love'—unless we are to restrict the word to a specialised behaviour pattern dependent on the particular institutions of matrimony and property of our period of history—is man's name for the emotional element in social relations. All languages and usages seem to agree in this, I love, *j'aime*, are expressions which may be used both for sexual and social emotions. The Freudian has an explanation for this, which we shall examine in a moment. If our definition of love is correct, it is true that love makes the world go round. But it would be rather truer to say that the society going round as it does, makes love what it is. This is one of those relations like that of knowing and being, which can only be understood in a dialectical manner. Thought guides action, yet it is action which gives birth to consciousness, and so the two separate, struggle, and return on each other, and therefore perpetually develop. Just as human life is being mingled with knowing, society is economic production mingled with love. This seems crude and even ludicrous to anyone accustomed to think of love as ethereal and in the soul, and economic production as base and earthly. But we love with our bodies and we eat and labour with our bodies, and deep love between two persons is generally distinguished from more transient forms of it by this test, that the two want to live together and thereafter function as one economic unit of society. As between the two, we know from biology that love, in its sexual form, appears before social economic production. But we also know that economic production in its primary individual form of metabolism, necessarily appears before love, for it is the essence of life. In the primitive cell metabolism exists before love has come into being. The cells at first multiply by fission, as a kind of surplus anabolism, and do not come together either in colonies (social behaviour) or fused in pairs for propagation (sexual behaviour). But because metabolism in the very dawn of life's history precedes the relation of love, it does not follow that love is a chance iridescence on life's surface. Metabolism, in the yet not fully understood affinity it demands among its protein molecules, already contains at a material level the rudiments of what men came to name Eros. Love must be implicit in matter.

Both popular and philosophic thought has recognised these deep foundations of love. Popular thought has given the same name to the affective tie that binds man and woman sexually, man and man in friendship, and parents and child in family relationships. A king's love for his people, a disciple's love for his teacher, an animal's love for its young and its master, have all been included in the one category in spite of obvious differences. It is no accident that all the great religions which have moved men's minds have spoken so much of love. Religions always drew their value and their power from their symbolisation of unconscious social relations, and, since social relations are mediated by love, it is always about love that religion is essentially talking when it utters fantasies about God, salvation, Heaven, Hell and grace. The mystics' claim *God is love*, and the hymn of St. Paul to love, are accurate statements of the valuable common content of all religions which in the past have been social forces. The Trinity, the cherubims, the Holy Souls in Purgatory, and the Communion of the Saints do not exist, and it did not really matter to men whether they existed, for in the past men have been content with Yahweh and Sheol, Buddha and Nirvana, Baal and Gilgamesh. What does matter to men is the emotional element in social relations, which these myths symbolise, and which makes man in each generation what he is. This emotion is not separate from but springs out of the economic basis of these relations, which thus determine religion. Man's quality in each age is determined by his emotional and technological relations, and these are not separate but part of the one social process.

The Freudian position is that all emotional relations

are simply variations of sexual love, cheated of their aim. That is why men call all varieties of tender relations 'love', because they are simply modified sexuality or diverted libido. Tenderness is inhibited sexuality. Although this view is attractive as a simplification, it is based on confused thinking. It assumes that there is a clear goal, sexual intercourse, and any love that does not achieve this goal is in some sense thwarted. This, however, presupposes something with this goal clearly in mind, and unless we believe in a god of love, this can only be the lover. But by definition the psyche whose inhibited sexuality is supposed to become love, is unconscious of the real goal. Take the example of infantile sexuality, an important part of Freud's theory of love. How can infantile affections be thwarted sexual love? On the one hand the infant, with no experience of sexual intercourse, cannot desire it consciously, and he cannot desire it unconsciously, i.e. somatically, because he has not the organs or reflexes for achieving sexual intercourse. Without the appropriate reflexes, sexual intercourse cannot exist for the unconscious. Its love therefore is of another kind—childish love. It is true that childish love is associated with zones many of which afterwards become sexually erotic, but that is only to say that man is material, that he has a body, and that this is used for contacts with other bodies. His contacts with other members of the world must be real physical contacts—mainly tactile when he is an infant, afterwards also visual and aural. Childish love is not thwarted sexual love, for the child neither knows sexual intercourse as an aim, nor is capable of it. It is childish love. That childish love is later to become sexual love is a truism. 'Thwarting' begs the question. Suppose, instead, Freud had said that infantile love was 'modified' adult love. We should at once have seen the fallacy. On the contrary it is adult sexual love which is 'modified' infantile love. It includes the more primitive behaviour pattern, but, as Freud admits, integrates it in a much more elaborate and powerful new system, due to the coming into being of the reflexes associated with sexual intercourse, the secondary sexual hormone, and all the qualitative changes in psychic orientation and content associated with puberty. Therefore Freud is standing love's development on its head. It would be precisely as accurate to regard the baby's body as a thwarted or inhibited adult body, as to regard the baby's affective life as that of a 'polymorphous perverse' adult.

In the same way the relation of a parent to an infant is not sexual love thwarted or inhibited. Sexual love is a behaviour-response, including a desire for sexual intercourse, evoked by certain stimuli. The infant is not a stimulus for this. It is very doubtful if the infant is primarily the stimulus for instinctive parental love at all. The phenomenon of 'false pregnancy' among bitches seems to prove the reverse. These animals develop after heat, in certain circumstances, maternal behaviour and emotion, without having become actually pregnant. To suppose that their maternal love is thwarted sexual love towards a non-existent puppy is to make psychology a comic opera. The parental love behaviour pattern varies widely from the sexual.

Again, the normal relations of friendship between persons of the same sex, in all their variety, from lasting and intimate friendship to a tenderness we feel for someone we have never seen merely because he is a fellow-countryman or a fellow-creature in distress, form a group of distinctive behaviour-patterns. It is unscientific to regard these as kinds of thwarted or inhibited sexual love. Indeed to do so robs the quite clear concept of sexual perversion of any meaning. In homosexuality or zoophily the sexual behaviour-emotion pattern is directed to abnormal objects, and is necessarily modified thereby. But if *all* tenderness for persons of one's own sex or animals, is simply the sexual pattern of behaviour modified by the novel circumstances, what is the difference? How can we distinguish between friendship and perversion? The error is due to a misunderstanding of what the instinct really is. An instinct is a certain innate behaviour-pattern or chain of reflexes, conditioned or modified by experience. The word 'love', as commonly used, includes such modified behaviour-patterns as delight in other peoples' presence, sensibility to one person rather than another, generosity towards them, desire to see them, and various other forms of affectionate behaviour which psychologists can only describe aridly and formally. It includes also the desire for sexual intercourse. Only behaviour-patterns of which this last is a component should be called sexual love, and to suppose that all the other forms of friendliness contain a suppressed desire for sexual intercourse, which is roughly the Freudian position, is to adopt the plan of the White Knight—

to dye one's whiskers green.
And then to use so large a fan
That they will not be seen.

Man, like all animals, is a creature whose innate behaviour-patterns are modified by experience, usually for 'the better', that is, so as to deal more expertly with reality. This process is called learning. We learn with our love responses as with others. To call this process inhibition or repression inverts the process of evolution.

Of course, sexual and friendly behaviour responses are very closely connected, and each pattern contains component parts common to both. But since one body, with one central nervous system, is common to all of one organism's behaviour, it is obvious that all its behaviour-patterns must contain a large number of common components. Running may, for example, in any animal, figure as part of sexual behaviour or as part of self-preservation (fear) behaviour. It does not follow that one instinct is the other, modified, repressed or inhibited.

As soon as we rid our mind of mythological entities of these separate instincts, like distinct souls, planted in the animal or human breast, we will be clearer on this point.

In 'the instincts', the savage soul—the little manikin dwelling in the marionette body and pulling the strings—has returned to psychology. With Freud this manikin, under the name of libido or eternal Eros, figures in the strangest way as a kind of symbolisation of bourgeois conceptions of liberty, like Rousseau's natural man. The unfortunate libido is exploited and oppressed and chained in the cruellest way by the structure of society and in its torments gives birth to all sociological and ideological phenomena. All this is simply a return to the old 'natural philosophy' conception of an indwelling vital force, with eternal desires and aims of its own.

This conception leads Freud to suppose that whatever a thing becomes, it remains the same thing inhibited or sublimated. This is to deny change. If soil becomes a rose, it is not just soil inhibited and sublimated. It is certainly still composed of the same elements, but it is also a rose, with its own character and qualities and laws. Even here Freud makes another error. If what is derived from a thing is nothing but that thing, we should not say that social relations are nothing but sexual relations; we should say that sexual love is nothing but social relations. In evolution primitive social relations precede primitive sexual relations if the following considerations are correct:

It is generally supposed that ontogenesis corresponds on the whole to phylogenesis. Before the infant achieves sexual love, it first experiences the simple metabolic relation between mother and fœtus, in which sexual love cannot be said to enter, for here there are no erotogenous zones. This is an economic relation between mother and child. The next step is infantile love, with erotogenous zones but not distinctively sexual behaviour. Finally, in the crisis of adolescence, the distinctive sexual reflexes appear. It will be argued that the sexual congress of ovum and spermatozoon precedes these stages. But these are protozoic relations, and man is metazoic. In the metazoa, sexual relations come after the simpler social relations of genesis and nurture.

In any case the same holds good of protozoa. The precedent condition of the congress of ovum and spermatozoon is the production of ova and spermatozoa. This is an asexual process and is part of the internal asexual economy of the cells of the body, bound together in a metabolism which is plainly economic. The relations of the primary sex cells are therefore asexual before they are sexual. But this is so with all protozoa, even those that do not become metazoa. Asexual relations between them always precede sexual, which grow out of them as a kind of late differentiation. Indeed this must plainly be the case. Before multiplication can proceed by sexual congress, there must be multiplication by fission, for you cannot, mathematically, get many out of one by fusion. Fission must come first, and fission demands a surplus anabolism which of itself implies a primitive economic basis. These considerations show clearly that, on the 'nothing but' basis, sexual love is *nothing but* social relations. But, of course, the 'nothing but' reduction is invalid. Sexual love is in mankind *something more* than the innate response that produces fusion between male and female cells. Social relations in humanity are something more than the metabolism that co-ordinates the cells of a metazoan, or a volvex colony. Passionate love and social altruism are the results of long periods of historical change, and the change is real, it is not just the old eternal entities wearing masks. But like a modern Parmenides, the instinct psychologist seems reluctant to recognise the reality of 'becoming'.

The simpler relations between cells, as evidenced in the ordinary metazoan body or the aggregations of asexual protozoa known as colonies, are primitive social or economic relations and form the basis from which human society's productive relations and forces have flowered. But it does not follow that they are the 'same thing' carried out in different media. They are what they are, subject to their own distinctive laws. What the individual body has in common with society is this: the relations between the cells of the human body are economic, there is division of labour, central control, exchange of products, and so forth. The one subordinates its interests, when required, to the whole. As in all socio-economic relations, the cells achieve more in unison than they do separately. But the body is subject to biological, society to sociological laws.

The sexual cells appear on the scene at puberty, when

the metazoan body has been a social entity for some time. Sexuality is therefore a kind of luxury, appearing at a late date, as a special modification of social-economic relations. *Sexual love is a modified economic relation.* Altruism, for example, is not, when exhibited socially, the result of an identification of one's self with the loved one, and therefore a special form of sexual love, as Freud suggests. Altruism, in its primitive and basic form of the sacrifice of one individual for others, appears long before sexual love, as part of the economic process of metabolism in the cells of the human body, unconnected with sexuality. But conscious altruism in a human being is not just the unconscious 'self-sacrifice' of a white corpuscle. It is a new quality, based on an old quantity. And sexual love is a new quality, differentiated out of the simpler socio-economic relations that preceded it.

Differentiation implies a difference. Although sexual love as a late development of socio-economic relations, gathers up within itself the qualities of its basis, it also contains something distinctively new. Sexual love is not a luxury, existing only for itself, but it returns again into the social relations from which it sprang, making them different to what they were. And, so changed, they in turn feed more richly the new thing rooted in them. Both reflect light on each other, for it is plain that sexual love, basically a chain of simple spinal reflexes, as shown by experiments on decerebrate guinea-pigs, has in humanity attracted to itself a number of economic relations and become enriched by them. The act of sexual intercourse need not involve this interweaving of relations, and in the lower organisms does not. Sexual intercourse need not be intertwined with the relations involved in the rearing of young, as in human family life, nor in the relations involved in earning one's living, keeping house, and making friends, as in human marriage. But because it is so intertwined, it is like a source of warmth irradiating these relations, and these in turn become fuel which feed it and bring about its enrichment and growth. The whole forms an elaborate system, part of the tapestry of society, and the richer pattern resulting from the mutual interweaving indicates that the Freudian conception of social relations as modified sexual love inverts the process of becoming.

The evolution of sexuality was of vital significance in the history of organisms. Primitive metabolic relations, such as those obtaining between the cells of metazoan bodies, are marked by a totalitarian ruthlessness in which the individual, as such, does not exist. The individual cell is completely subordinated to the organism as a whole. This is necessarily the case, because the cell is not yet an individual in its own right, but simply a part of the parent cell which has become differentiated and detached. This involves an almost exact likeness to the parent cell, so that such cells, as long as they continue to be capable of fission, have a kind of immortality, the children being almost exactly the same as the parents. It is also correspondingly difficult for the new to come into being.

Generation after generation repeats the same pattern. All defects are reproduced. The parent cell has eaten sour grapes, and therefore the grandchildren's teeth are necessarily set on edge.

The coming of sexuality breaks the stale routine of habit. It is therefore the genesis of individuality within the ambit of society. Something distinctively new now comes into being, because the child will no longer resemble either parent exactly but, by combining a selection of the genes from both, will be someone different from either. Moreover, each child, with a different selection of genes, will be slightly different, and thus bad qualities may be weeded out by natural selection. Not all the children's teeth are set on edge. The range of qualities in the offspring is increased. Some, it is true, will be far worse than the offspring of an asexual parent, for they will unite the defects of both parents, but others will be better, and natural selection will have a wider range of varieties to work on. It is as if good has come into the world by the generation of evil, and if we take seriously the identity of opposites, must not this be the case?

At the same time death has come into the world. Love, the giver of individuality, is also the giver of death, the antithesis of personality. That is why the life-instinct and the death-instinct, Eros and Thanatos, seem so closely united, not as Freud thought because they are specific instincts, but because death defines love. The immortality of primitive cells, secured by simple fission, vanishes when they conjugate and spawn. The parents now live in their children only in a provisional half-hearted manner.

This is a kind of price that life pays for greater difference, for becoming life as we understand it. For greater richness and complexity, hastening the hand of time, we pay the priceless coin of Death. To their children, no longer simple buds of themselves, the individual cells can bequeath more abundant life and greater differentiation but only by sinking half their genetic share in them and giving up their near immortality. Only with this advent of sexual love and real death can one talk about 'personalities' and 'individuals'; other cells are buds. The birth of a new personality demands the death of the old. This 'I' that dies is created by death.

In its appearance, none the less, sexual love is selfish. Sexual cells reject the colonial and social tie of asexual reproduction in favour of an intimate exclusive tie between two of them alone. They are luxurious cells, playing no part in the economic production of the metazoan body. And, similarly, in social life sexual love has a selfish aspect. The lovers turn away from the community; their demand is to be alone, to be by themselves, to enjoy each other. Thus sexual love appears as a dissolving power in society.

The social asexual cell is strictly subordinated to the plan of the organism. It works tirelessly, secreting or vibrating or dying for the good of the community. Beside it the sexual cell seems, in the community, like the selfish hedonist beside the devoted hard-working celibate. The sexual cell is responding with all its being to something which allures merely by the satisfaction it gives to the individual. Love, even in its other-regarding aspect, seems a kind of giant selfishness projected on the beloved. But this is not the whole truth. This same selfish cell brings to birth something which is unknown before—individuality. The cell, temporarily released from the iron plan of organic metabolism by the invention of sexuality, is by this act enriched in behaviour. It is the beginning of that individuation which in man leads to consciousness. The sexual behaviour brings a new pattern into life. On the one hand the sexual cells, ignoring the demands of 'society', are thereby led to enrich and complicate their self-hood. More importantly, this very sexual partnership involves eventually the annihilation of both personalities in the birth of the new individualities, whose characters will be formed from a selection of the genes of both parents, and therefore different from either. The self-sacrificing cell enjoys the possibility of a perpetual immortality as a reward for its self-sacrifice. The sexual cell buys its one brief hour of glorious life, for an age without a name, and yet, by that very death and life, it has given rise to the potentialities of individualism.

This, however, is too anthropomorphic a way of looking at it. As long as asexuality prevails, it is not possible to talk about individuality at all. Are the leaves of one tree individual? No, they are part of the one tree. In the same way the cells of the metazoan body are all part of each other though spatially separate. They are formed from each other by simple fission. Therefore neither the question of self-sacrifice nor immortality arise. The asexual cell has no 'self' to sacrifice and immortality is meaningless except in the sense that all matter is immortal. Immortality is meaningless without *personal* immortality, and the asexual cell has no personality.

Immortality is not a superior kind of mortality, a life protracted to infinity, an endless personal survival. It is the primitive state from which both mortality and personality arose. If the concept of life to us is almost meaningless except as the life of an individual, we must say that death gave rise to life; both are aspects of the same movement of differentiation. All craving for immortality, so human and so understandable, is yet a craving for a regression, for a return to primitive unconscious being, to shift off ourselves the heavy responsibilities of consciousness, love and individuality. All conceptions of immortality as endless survivals of personalities walking about in familiar surroundings strike the mind with a strange sense of unreality. The only conceptions of immortality which seem reasonable, even if impossible, are the Buddhist and Hindoo conceptions of immortality as a merging of oneself into the absolute, Nirvana, a beingless primitive sleep. And this is what immortality is, a return to the blind unconscious regression of primitive being, back farther still to the timelessness of immortal matter. Because life, faced with any difficult situation, always tends to wish to relapse to a solution achieved at an earlier stage of development, this concept of immortality makes an appeal to man particularly in periods of inferiority or depression.

This concern with immortality is not so much a fear of death as a special kind of defeatist resignation to it, as in late Egypt and the Oriental mystery cults. A *faint* belief or *complete disbelief* in immortality, so far from begetting a resignation to death, necessarily produces a vigorous dislike of it. All beaten, depressed and terrified people, all slave and expropriated classes, turn to another immortal timeless life for consolation. Biological immortality, splitting into personality and death, generates two opposites which repel each other ; the more full and abundant our life, the more we are repelled by death, and this repulsion, so painful, is yet productive of pleasure, for it forces us to cram our now valued lives full of richness and complexity, to seize great armfuls of time and action, to achieve and conquer and love and suffer before we die. Death, the negation of life, thus generates it. All spring, all youth, all health yields its peculiar and rich savour just because of this, that they go :

And at my back I always hear,
Time's winged chariot hastening near.

. . . .

Human society is distinguished from the simple metabolic society of somatic cells because it is more than metabolic, it is also individualistic. The individual, apparently opposed to society, yet gives society its inner driving power, and society by its internal development itself brings about the individuation of its units.

Insect society here contrasts with human. There has been a regression to a relative immortality. The workers have all been desexualised. They have lost their individuality and regressed almost to the status of somatic cells. The strange rapport between members of a hive or formicary is not surprising when we think of them as virtually all parts of the one body, daughter cells of the queen. But this same regression and de-individuation produces stagnation as compared with human society. All powers of change and individualism are concentrated in the genetic change of the few sexual members. It is therefore a slow change. Insect societies have almost ceased to live. Immune from the changing and yet living hand of time, they have achieved some of the dull immortality of the diamond.

In human society, however, the endless war between individual and economic relations, between love and metabolism, is the source of endless social advance. Sexuality, because it gave rise to individuality, also helped to give rise to consciousness. Metabolism (or productive forces) changes from age to age, and this change imposes a tension upon productive relations. But this strife, extending throughout society, is felt in a characteristic form in the sphere of man's feeling, in his consciousness, for consciousness is basically affective. It is felt as if outside forces in society are starving or thwarting men's emotional lives, as if life is becoming glamourless or cruel. For the productive relations are social relations and conscious tenderness is generated in them.

Sexual love itself is continually enriched and changed by economic relations, at the same time as economic relations gain new warmth and complexity from love. To every stage of economic development corresponds a richer, subtler, more sensitive behaviour-pattern associated with sexual love. To bourgeois culture belongs passionate love, to feudal romantic or chivalrous love, and to slave-owning Greek culture Platonic love.

To our generation the association of economic relations with sexual love seems arbitrary, not because our idea of love is too rich but because our notion of economic relations is too bourgeois. Bourgeois civilisation has reduced social relations to the cash nexus. They have become emptied of affection. To a psychologist, the whole world seems suffering from a starvation of love, and this need appears in a compensatory and pathological form as neurosis, hate, perversion, and unrest.

Even to-day, in those few economic relations which still survive in a pre-bourgeois form, we can see tenderness as the essence of the relation. The commodity fetishism which sees in a relation between *men* only a relation between *things* has not yet dried it up. The economic relation of the mother to her fœtus, of the child to the parent and *vice versa*, retains its primitive form to show this clearly. We can see fainter traces in the relation of master to pupil, of governess to child, household servant to master or mistress, and the few surviving examples of a feudal relation between master and man.

Where can this tenderness be found in the characteristically bourgeois relations our culture substitutes for them—the relations of capitalist and labourer; hotel servant and guest; company promoter and shareholder; correspondence-course writer and mug? This tenderness, expelled from all other relations, is collected and utilised to-day in a vague mystical manner as the binding force for the one social relation of 'being in the same State'. This is a genuine social relation, that of being in the fabric of coercion exploited by one ruling class, but it is not one which in its named form is likely to produce tenderness. It is therefore necessary to substitute for the naked relation a fictional one—a fictitious 'race', a wonderful happy family, or a dummy King or Leader whose wisdom and statesmanship and character are regarded as semi-divine, even where his position is constitutionally that of a rubber stamp. By this means a powerful '*participation mystique*' is secured. As Fascism and Nazism show, the more violent the exploitation, the more ardent and mythological the patriotism; the more heartless and unemotional the relations, the more the parade of hypocritical feeling. This is characteristic of developed bourgeois relations. In primitive relations among a group, as the researches of anthropologists show, economic production is inextricably interwoven with social affection. Between tribes, between chief and subject, or between different members of a group, the economic relation figures as an exchange of gifts, as a tribute of affection in the literal sense. It is the love that goes with the gifts, which is the giving, is the vital economic thing. Many primitive transactions which to the early bourgeois observer seemed to be bourgeois exchange, that is, the getting of as much as possible for as little as possible, are now, by more searching observers, discovered to be the very opposite, each side trying to embarrass the other by a superfluity of gifts. The Melanesian's pride is found to be in his having contributed more yams than anyone else to his maternal uncle or chief. At the potlatch, the North American Indian demonstrates his social value by impoverishing himself. This conception of economic relation as tender relation, and a fit medium for generosity and altruism, appears in barbaric and even feudal relations. We must not idealise them, or imagine that simple savage tenderness is the same as the more developed, subtle and sophisticated emotion we feel. But it is equally wrong, by wresting and straining the facts, to give a bourgeois cynical interpretation to the different primitive economic relations of agriculture, hunting and land tenure among the primitive African, American and Oceanic races.

In all the distinctive bourgeois relations, it is characteristic that tenderness is completely expelled, because tenderness can only exist between men, and in capitalism all relations appear to be between a man and a commodity.

The relation of the guildsman to his journeyman, the slave-owner to his plantation slave, the lord to his serf, the king to his subjects, was a relation between man and man, and although it was a relation, not of co-operation but of domination and submission, of exploiter and exploited, it was a human relation. It was unpleasantly like the relation of a man and his dog, but at least it was tender. How can even that much consideration enter into the relations of a group of shareholders to the employees of a limited liability company? Or between Indian coolies and British tea drinkers? Or between a bourgeois bureaucracy and the proletariat?

In bourgeois relations the sole recognised legal social relation among adults is the contract, considered as damnifiable in cash. Nothing can be enforced upon a man but the payment of money; even marriage can be escaped from by a suitable cash compensation. Man is completely free except for the payment of money. That is the overt character of bourgeois relations. Secretly it is different, for society can only be a relation between men, not between man and a thing, not even between man and cash. Bourgeois society thinks that is the relation on which it turns, but, as Marx showed, in bourgeois society it is still a relation between men, between exploiters and exploited. It is the vehicle of a specific type of exploitation. The bourgeois dream is that by substituting this relation to a thing for feudal slave-owning or primitive relations between men, man becomes completely free. But this is an illusion. Since man only becomes free through social relations, this means that the bourgeois shuts his eyes to facts. For conscious planned social relations he substitutes unconscious unplanned social relations which, like all unconscious forces, work blindly and disastrously.

None the less, the bourgeois was determined to believe that the market was the only social relation between man and man. This meant that he must refuse to believe that love was an integral part of a social relation. He repressed this tenderness from his social consciousness. In its final form this becomes the treason of man to his capacity for love, the appearance of love in the form of neurosis, hate, and fantasy, which the psycho-analysts discover everywhere in bourgeois man. In one sense the Married Woman's Property Act was a charter of freedom for women. In another sense it was merely a charter of bourgeois repression, a recognition that the economic relations between husband and wife were no longer tender but merely cash.

In their early stages bourgeois relations, by intensifying individualism, give a special heightening to sexual love. Before they crystallise out as relations to cash, bourgeois social relations simply seem to express man's demand for freedom from obsolete social bonds, and this demand for individuality is then a progressive force. Sexual love now takes on, as clearly seen in art, a special value as the expression *par excellence* of individuality. We have the emergence of that characteristic achievement of bourgeois culture, passionate love, conceived as both romantic and sensual, whereas neither Greek nor mediæval culture could conceive romantic and sensual love except as exclusive opposites. Passionate love contributes new overtones to feeling and conscious life. Moreover, this demand for individuality was also enriching other forms of love, as long as it was revolutionary and creative. It gave men a new tenderness towards each other, conceived as a tenderness of each other's liberty, of each other's personal worth. Thus bourgeois culture in its springtime gave birth to passionate sexual love, and a tenderness for the 'liberty'—the individual outline—of other members of society. Both these are genuine enrichments, which civilisation cannot now lose.

None the less, the contradiction in bourgeois social relations, that private advantage is common weal, that freedom is sought individually *and* anti-socially, necessarily revealed its nature in due course. Man cannot exist without relations to other men, and the bourgeois demand that he should do so merely meant that these relations were disguised as a relation to commodities. As this developing relation produced industrial capitalism and the modern bourgeois State, it sucked the tenderness out of all social relations. Ultimately it even affected sexual love itself, and began to take from it the very enrichments sexual love had derived from tender social relations. Passionate bourgeois love is to-day like a flower which is being stripped of its petals one by one. These petals are the patterns of behaviour derived from bourgeois social relations, which had been transferred to sexual love and been transformed and warmed by it, just as the flower's colourful petals consist of converted green leaves. In the institution of bourgeois marriage, these economic relations—the *individual* family, the *personal* income—were warmed by sexual love into something of nobility. True, bourgeois social relations, even when so transformed, retained some of their ugly untender character. The man too often regards love as similar to a bourgeois property relation, as a relation between a man and a thing and not between man and man. The wife was his property for life. She had to be beautiful to gratify his acquisitive instincts ; faithful because a man's property must not alienate itself from him ; but he, the owner, can be unfaithful, because he can acquire other property without affecting his present holding. A similar relation imposed itself on the children he had fed and clothed, and therefore paid their wages. They had sold their labour power to him. In Roman slave-owning civilisation, the child's legal position appears as that of slave to the father, and moreover a slave incapable of manumission. But even slavery is a relation between men. These ugly possessive features of bourgeois social relations always gave bourgeois love a selfish jealous undertone, which the bourgeois, despite the researches of anthropology, considers as instinctive and natural. Private property was not invented by bourgeoisdom. It is a potentiality of man's nature, or it could never have appeared in bourgeoisdom. But bourgeoisdom was its flowering, its elevation and the prime motive power of social relations; and the flavour accordingly pervades all bourgeois life.

With the exhaustion of bourgeois social relations, bourgeois passionate love begins also to wither before the economic blast. On the one hand marriage has become increasingly 'expensive'. It must be put off till late life. That marriage—which for bourgeois culture and particularly for the woman had been the most valued pattern of love behaviour—is to-day only a late and specialised variety of it. Children are increasingly expensive, and the tender social relations associated with them more rarely form part of the standard marriage pattern. From these and other causes that elaborate and complex creation, passionate bourgeois love is more and more being stripped of its corolla and reverting to a primitive form of fugitive sexual intercourse. This, the inevitable consequence of the exhaustion of bourgeois social relations, is denounced as 'Sin', the 'levity of the young', 'the breakdown of the institution of marriage', 'growing promiscuity', the 'result of birth-control', and so on. But all this abuse is beside the point. Passionate bourgeois love really prepared its own death. The same causes which caused its flowering in course of time brought about this withering.

To-day love could prepare an appalling indictment of the wrongs and privations that bourgeois social relations have inflicted upon it. The misery of the world is economic, but that does not mean that it is cash. That is a bourgeois error. Just because they are economic, they involve the tenderest and most valued feelings of social man. For the satisfaction of all the rich emotional capabilities and social tenderness of which bourgeois relations have deprived him, man turns vainly to religion, hate, patriotism, fascism, and the sentimentality of films and novels, which paint in imagination loves he cannot experience in life. Because of this he is neurotic, unhappy, sick, liable to the mass-hatreds of war and anti-semitism, to absurd and yet pathetic Royal Jubilee or Funeral enthusiasms and to mad impossible loyalties to Hitlers and Aryan grandmothers. Because of this life seems to him empty, stale, and unprofitable. Man delights him not, nor woman neither.

Bourgeois social relations, by transforming in this way all tender relations between men to relations to commodities, prepare their own doom. The threads that bind feudal lord to liege, chief to tribe, patriarch to household slave, father to son, because they are tender are strong. But those that bind shareholder to wage-employee, civil servant to taxpayer, and all men to the impersonal market, because they are merely cash and devoid of tender relations, cannot hold. The chief's laws are understandable. The fiat of a man god is still a personal and affectionate command.

But the laws of supply and demand (their substitute in bourgeois culture) are without any power save blind compulsion. To-day it is as if love and economic relations have gathered at two opposite poles. All the unused tenderness of man's instincts gather at one pole and at the other are economic relations, reduced to bare coercive rights to commodities. This polar segregation is the source of a terrific tension, and will give rise to a vast transformation of bourgeois society. They must, in a revolutionary destruction and construction, return in on each other and fuse in a new synthesis. This is communism.

Thus the forces that produce communism can be viewed from two aspects. From the quantitative aspect, productive forces, which have outgrown bourgeois social relations, burst those fetters. But the fight is fought to an issue in men's consciousness. Man, the individual, feels the outmoding of these relations, their sloughing by reality, as the death of all that is valuable to him. The demand to bring back to consciousness these vanished values appears as hate for the present and love for the new, the dynamic power of revolution. Emotion bursts from the ground in which it has been repressed with all the force of an explosion. The whole structure of society is shattered. This is a revolution.

VII

FREUD

A STUDY IN BOURGEOIS PSYCHOLOGY

FREUD is certain to be remembered and honoured as one of the pioneers of scientific psychology. But it is probable that like Kepler he will be regarded as a scientist who discovered important empirical facts but was unable to synthesise these discoveries except in a primitive semi-magical framework. Kepler with his divine Sun God, lived in the religious age of physics, Freud for all his honesty lives in the mythical era of psychology:

'It may now be expected that the other of the "two heavenly forces", eternal Eros, will put forth his strength so as to maintain himself alongside of his equally immortal adversary.'

This is Freud's prognosis of the future of our civilisation. It is no bad symbolisation of the psychological trend of the present, but it will be seen that it is mythological symbolisation. Examination of the remainder of his psychology shows that it is generally religious in its presentation. It is a psychology of forces and personifications. Freud is no exceptional psychologist here. Psychology still awaits its Newton. At least Freud has refused to accept the outworn shams of Christianity or of idealistic metaphysics. In *The Future of an Illusion* he maintains the fruitful materialistic traditions of bourgeois science, which bourgeois science itself to-day as it loses its grip is deserting. The metaphysical psychology with its memory, reason, conation, perception, thought and feeling which Freud helped to destroy is more mythological than Freudism. This psychology, of which Freudism is an enemy, belongs to an even earlier age of science. It reduces mentation to verbiage, and then the organisation of this verbiage is called thought. It is, however, real mentation with which Freud deals always, only he symbolises the inner structure of this neurological behaviour in terms of real entities as glamorous and personal as the Olympian gods of old. The Censor, the Ego, the Super-ego, the Id, the Oedipus complex, and the Inhibition are mind-deities, like the weather deities who inhabited Greek Olympus. Freud's picture of a struggle between eternal Eros and eternal Thanatos, between the life and death instincts, between the reality principle and the pleasure principle, is only the eternal dualism of reflective barbarians, carried over by Christianity from Zoroastrianism, and now introjected by Freud into the human mind. It represents a real struggle but in terms of a Western bourgeois myth.

As confirmation of his fable about Zeus, the Greek could point to the thunder and lightning. As confirmation of the endless war between Ormuzd and Ahriman, the Parsee could remind the sceptic of the endless warfare that tears life in twain. Freudians point to the psychic phenomena of dreams, hysteric and neurotic symptoms, obsessions and slips of the pen and tongue as confirmation of their intricate mythology. The early scientists could claim the fall of every stone as the evidence of the mysterious force of gravity and all phenomena of heat and cold as testimony to the passage of a mysterious 'caloric'. In Freudism 'libido' plays the part of the mythical 'caloric' of eighteenth-century heat mechanics, or of the 'gravity' of Newtonian physics.

It may be urged with some reason that psychology is an appropriate sphere for fables and emotive symbolisation, but this claim withdraws it from the circle of science to that of art. It is better to demand that mythical psychology should exist only in the novel and that psychology should be a science. If so, the obligation falls upon psychoanalysts either to leave any empirical facts they have discovered in thin air for some abler mind to fit into a causal scheme, as Newton correlated Kepler's separate and arbitrary laws of planetary motion, or else they must clearly exhibit the causality of their discoveries without recourse to mythological entities. This Freud and his followers have failed to do. Thus instead of being causal and materialistic, their psychology is religious and idealistic. Yet Freud is a materialist and is clearly aware of the illusory content of religion. But he is also a bourgeois. This class outlook affects his psychology through certain implicit assumptions from which he starts, assumptions that appear in all bourgeois culture as a disturbing yet invisible force, just as Uranus until discovered was for us only a mysterious perturbation in the orbits of the known planets. These implicit assumptions are firstly that the consciousness of men is *sui generis*, unfolding like a flower from the seed instead of being a primarily social creation, and secondly that there is a source of free action in the individual, the 'free will', the 'wish', or the 'instincts', which is only free in proportion to the extent to which it is unrestrained by social influences. These two assumptions are of vital significance for psychology, and just because they are implicit, they act like buried magnets, distorting all Freud's psychology and making it an unreal kind of a science tainted with wish-fulfilment.

Freud has been exceptionally unfortunate in that his school of psychology has been rent repeatedly by schisms. Jung and Adler are the most notable schismatics, but almost every psychoanalyst is a heretic in embryo. Now this must necessarily have been a matter for sorrow to Freud although he has borne it as calmly as he has borne the numerous attacks from all with vested interests in contemporary morality whom his discoveries seemed to menace. The Freudian schisms are not paralleled in other sciences. The disciples of a discoverer of new empirical principles, such as the disciples of Darwin, Newton and Einstein, do not as a rule turn and rend him. They work within the general limits of his formulations, merely enrichening and modifying them, without feeling called upon to attack the very foundations on which the structure is based.

Freud is himself indirectly to blame. Schism is the hall-mark of religion, and a man who treats scientific facts as does Freud, in a religious way, must necessarily expect the trials and tribulations, as well as the intense personal relationships, of a religious leader. In approaching science in a religious spirit, I do not mean in a 'reverent' spirit. The scientist necessarily approaches reality, with all its richness and complexity, with a feeling of reverence and insignificance which is the more intense the more materialistic he is, and, the less he feels that this reality is a mere offshoot or emanation of a Divine friend of his. I mean by a 'religious' approach, the belief that scientific phenomena are adequately explained by any symbolisation which includes and accounts for the phenomena. Thus 'caloric' accounts for temperature phenomena. None the less, no such mysterious stuff exists. In the same way Freud supposes that any fable which includes a connected statement of genuine psychical phenomena is a scientific hypothesis, whether or no it exhibits in a causal manner the inner relations of the phenomena. Of course such explanations break down because they do not fit into the causal scheme of science as a whole.

Now this is precisely the way religion sets about explaining the world, thunder and lightning are caused by deities. The world exists because it was created by a God. Disaster is the will of an omnipotent deity, or the triumph of an evil deity over an omnipotent deity. We die because we sinned long ago. Moreover, religion naïvely supposes that the fact that there is thunder and lightning, that the world exists, that disaster occurs in it, and that we die, is a proof that deities exist, that God created the world, and that we sinned long ago. This is what theologians mean by the Cosmological and Teleological proofs of God's existence. But this kind of 'proof' was long ago banished from science, and it is strange to see a man of Freud's intellectual gifts impressed by it. It is a sign of the crisis reached in bourgeois culture when psychology cannot escape from this kind of thing.

It follows from presuming that an adequate explanation of certain facts will be furnished by any fable connecting these facts, that for any group of facts an indefinite number of myths can be advanced as an explanation. Thus an indefinite number of religions exist which explain with different myths the same facts of man's unhappiness, his cruelty, his aspirations, his sufferings, his inequality and his death. Religion by its method of approach spawns schisms. The only reason that Churches can exist without disintegration is because of their material foundations in the social relations of their time.

Science can recognise only explanations which with as little symbolisation as possible exhibit the mutual determination of the phenomena concerned, and their relation with the rest of reality. Thus one scientific hypothesis is intolerant. It drives out another.

Scientific explanations, because of their austere structure, are not equally good, as different religions are equally good. One or other must go to the wall. And the test is simple. If, of two hypotheses one exhibits more comprehensively and less symbolically the structure of the determinism of the phenomena it explains and their relation to the already established structure of reality, that hypothesis will be more powerful as an instrument for predicting the recurrence of such phenomena in real life. Hence arises the crucial test, which decides between one hypothesis and another. For example, the crucial tests of the Einstein theory, as compared with the Newtonian, were the bending of light, the perturbation of planetary orbits, the increase of mass of alpha particles, and the shifts of the spectra of receding stars. But it is never possible to demonstrate by a crucial test the rival truths of the Protestant and Catholic theories, simply because they deal with entities assumed to be outside the structure of determined reality. The crucial test of the two theories is presumed to occur at the Last Judgment, that is, never in this life. The theories are expressly so formulated that it is not, for example, possible to test the Eucharist by chemical analysis. The Catholic theory states that in being turned into Christ's body the bread retains all the chemical and physical properties of ordinary bread. In the same way the Protestant theory makes it pointless to test for the salvation of a soul, precisely because the soul is asserted to be completely non-material and therefore inaccessible to determinism.

No hypothesis, religious or scientific, can have any

meaning unless it can give rise to a crucial test, which will enable it to be socially compared with other hypotheses. Thought must interact with external reality to be of value or significance. Capitalist and socialist economists dispute as meaninglessly as theologians as long as they base their defences of the rival systems on justice, liberty, man's natural equality, or any other 'rights'. No one has yet devised an instrument to measure or determine justice, equality, or liberty. The Marxian can be concerned only with the structure of concrete society and he will on this basis advance socialism as a superior form of organisation at a certain period of history because it permits a more efficient use of the means of material production. This makes possible the crucial test of practice—is communism more productive than capitalism? Thus economics remains scientific because it remains in the sphere of reality and does not deal with entities that cannot be determined quantitively. For this reason, historical materialism has not given rise to as many brands of socialism as there are theorists. It can only be opposed by an hypothesis more penetrative of reality. The 'cast-iron inflexible dogmatism' of the communist corresponds to the scientists' 'rigid' and universal adherence to a methodological principle, such as the conservation of energy, until a fresh hypothesis, capable of a crucial test, has shown the need for its expansion or modification.

When we see a scientific 'school' rent by schism, or engaged in vigorous persecution, we may assume that a certain amount of the religious spirit has entered its science. Science has never been wholly free of it, but it has rent psychoanalysis into fragments.

Adler, Freud and Jung deal with the same mental phenomena. They are as follows: Psychic phenomena consist of innervations of some of which we, as subjects, have a privileged (subjective) view. Some of these innervations, the smallest and most recent group phylogenetically, form a group often called the consciousness, the ego, or the subject. This group appears to be more self-determined than the other groups but all affect each other and form a kind of hierarchic process. Those which do not form part of the consciousness are called unconscious. At the moment of birth the neurones capable of innervation exhibit certain specific patterns of innervation, involving certain specific somatic behaviour, as a result of internal and external stimuli. These patterns are known as 'the instincts'. But the experience resulting from the awakening of these patterns modifies, by means of a phenomenon which may be called *memory* but is not peculiar to consciousness, the patterns themselves. At any moment of time, therefore, the system as a whole has a slightly different resonance or totality of patterns as a result of previous behaviour due to the then totality of patterns. The result will be to increase with lapse of time the range and complexity of the behaviour response to reality, and the hierarchy of groups of possible innervation combinations. We say, therefore, in ordinary language, that in the course of life a man learns by experience, or, a little more technically, that his instincts are modified or conditioned by situations. Such expressions contain a certain amount of mythology, perhaps at present unavoidable. In particular the more autonomous group called the 'consciousness', in whose language all explanations of other less autonomous groups must be phrased, will necessarily tend to write everything from its angle, and give a peculiar twist to the description. Science itself is a product of consciousness.

Experiment leads us to believe that the innervations concerned in consciousness are phylogenetically the most recent in evolution, and that the older the neurone groups, the less modifiable they are in their behaviour, i.e. the less they are able to 'learn' by 'experience'. Hence they may be described as more infantile, primitive, bestial, archaic or automatic, according to the mythological language one is adopting at the time.

In every innervation, however simple, the whole system of neurones is really concerned. If we play a chord on the piano, the strings we do not strike are as much concerned as those we do, because the chord is what it is being part of the well-tempered scale, and to the chord contribute also the wood, the air of the room, and our ears. Though consciousness deals with psychic phenomena in its own terms, yet in all conscious phenomena the innervations of the rest of the system are concerned and their innate responses, modified or unmodified, give all behaviour, including conscious phenomena, the 'ground' of their specific pattern. Hence we may say that the Unconscious modifies all behaviour, including consciousness; that is, that unconscious innervation and experience are a part of consciousness.

The study of this modification of the consciousness by the unconscious is naturally of great interest to our consciousness. To understand it we must know accurately the innate responses of all parts of the nervous system, and the laws of their harmony. Sometimes as a result of the temporary instability of the conscious innervation pattern (e.g. in situations of emergency or difficulty or in sleep), the tune of behaviour is called chiefly by the phylogenetically older neurones, and these, as we saw, were less teachable than the newer groups. We then have behaviour in which there is a return to the earlier and less experienced state, the so-called infantile regression. In it some of life's experience is thrown away. We may also call this behaviour instinctive.

Now these disturbances have been studied by Freud, and he has made some interesting empirical discoveries about them. He has shown how much more common they are than we suspect and has elaborated a technique for detecting them. All his discoveries have been embodied in an elaborate and ingenious myth, or series of myths. This is due partly to the fact that he has not taken his own doctrine seriously. He has not realised that, since it is consciousness which is formulating psychoanalysis, all unconscious phenomena are likely to appear as seen by consciousness, not as causal phenomena with the same physiological basis as consciousness and ultimately homogeneous with it, but as wicked demons which burst into the neat ordered world of consciousness. Just as causal phenomena, such as thunder and lightning, which burst into the accustomed world of the primitive, were attributed to the arbitrary acts of deities, so unconscious 'influences', causing perturbations in the conscious world, are by Freud called by such rude names as distortion, inhibition, regression, obsession, the id, the censor, the pleasure-principle, Eros, libido, the death instinct, the reality principle, a complex, a compulsion. Freud does not perceive the implications of the physiological content of his theory. All innervation patterns consist of an innate response (instinct) modified by experience (inhibition), and thus all innervation patterns contain varying proportions of conscious and unconscious elements, connected in various ways, but all forming the one circuit, overtly visible in behaviour. Freud has accepted for this part of his theory the prejudiced view of consciousness. He treats all unconscious components of behaviour as perturbations, distortions, or interferences, just as the treble part in music might regard the bass as distortion by some primitive unconsciousness. Just as mythological and consistent a psychology as Freud's might be written from the point of view of the 'unconscious' in which, instead of the 'instincts', the 'experiences' would now play the part of energetic imprisoned demons distorting or inhibiting the stability and simple life of the innate responses. And, in fact, when Freud comes to treat civilisation and man as a whole, he does swing over to this point of view. It is now experience or consciousness (culture) which is thwarting or distorting instinct (the unconscious). Naturally, therefore, Freud's doctrine contains a dualism which *cannot* be resolved.

But of course both consciousness and unconsciousness, as sharply distinct entities, are abstractions. In all the innervations which are part of behaviour, a varying proportion make up the group which at any time we call the consciousness or the ego. And they are not separate ; consciousness is made vivid and given its content by the unconscious innervations, whose contribution we know consciously only as affect. A thought without affect is unconscious ; it is simply one of the cortical neurones mnemically modified, but not at that moment affectively glowing, and therefore not part of the live circuit of unconsciousness. It is only an unconscious memory. Equally an unconscious innervation or affect without memory is not an affect at all, but simply an instinctive reflex, a tendency unmodified by experience. Consciousness and unconsciousness are not exclusive opposites, but in any hierarchy of innervations forming the behaviour of the moment we have a certain amount with high mnemic modifiability and others with high innate predisposition, and the proportion of these may be varying. But they are in mutual relation, like the positive and negative poles of a battery activating a circuit, and it is only by abstraction that we separate out the complex called consciousness, as we might separate out the threads forming the pattern on a tapestry. The same threads pass through to the other side and form the reverse pattern there, the unconscious, and each pattern determines the other.

Freud gave to these discoveries of his, which were founded on the previous work of Charcot, Janet, Morton Prince, and Bleuler, formulations drawn from his consciousness, without the rigorous causality demanded in physical or chemical hypotheses. As a result Freud's terminology consists of little but the abusive names coined by the consciousness for its distortion by the unconscious, or of the pitiful complaints by the unconscious of its modification by the experience embodied in conscious innervations. On the whole our sympathies will be with the consciousness, for the consciousness represents recent experience, and recent experience is the richest ; but reality reminds us that we cannot simply live in the new experience of the present. If we do, we shall be unable to advance beyond it ; we shall be trapped in the limitations of the present. We must accept the present more thoroughly than that, we must accept the past *included* in the present. That does not mean that we must accept the past as the past, for, in being included in the present, it is changed. That indeed is what each present *is* in relation to the precedent past, it is that precedent past modified by the impression of an additional experience ; and that present itself becomes the past when it is synthesised in a new present. This may sound metaphysical, and yet in the human body we see it given a 'crude' and material physiological basis. Everything below the optic thalamus represents the inherited experience of the ancestral past. The cerebrum is the organ for storing each present as it becomes the past, and sensory perception is the process by which the past, acquiring new experience, becomes the present. This ingression gives rise to the will, to the future.

Thus though we accept consciousness as latest and richest, we must not reject the Unconscious, as the worship of the consciousness may too easily lead us to do. Those who accept consciousness only are entrapped in immediate experience, and can never progress to a richer consciousness ; just as those who ignore the past in the present in the form of history are unable to grasp the richer future, which they write only in terms of the barren present. This is the lesson of historical materialism, that the future is not contained in the present, but in the present *plus* the past.

Still less can we accept *only* the past. That is worse than the other, it is a return to outworn things, it is infantile regression. It is the path that perpetually appeals to man when, as to-day, his consciousness seems to fail him at the tasks with which he is faced, but it is the way of defeat. The Unconscious has its wisdom, certainly, for it contains the condensed experience of ages of evolution, stamped in by natural selection. Our life is built on the foundations of the somatic wisdom of unconscious innervations. None the less, the spear-point of life's insertion into the reality is the present, it is new experience and this new experience is unseizable by unconsciousness. It *is* consciousness.

Freudism does not accept the story of one party to

the exclusion of the other's. It accepts *both* uncritically, and so involves itself in an irreconcilable dualism. After showing how the wicked complex-devils of the Unconscious distort and obsess the consciousness, Freud goes over to the other side and paints the Unconscious as it would like to paint itself. He shows us the Instincts tortured by the inhibitions of culture, martyrs to the present and to consciousness. Yet the scientist ought in these matters to be impartial, otherwise he will never synthesise these two opposites, past and present, new and old. Freud raises only the barren trichotomy of metaphysics: (i) infantile regression (or worship of the past); (ii) conservatism (or blind acceptance of the present); (iii) dualism (the conception of present and past as eternal antagonists). Only the man who sees how the past is included in the present, can proceed to the future, child of a 'Marriage of Heaven and Hell'. They are included in the primary process of becoming, exhibited in the organism as active behaviour, in which unconscious and conscious innervations are the bass and treble of the innervation harmony in whose theme we distinguish instinct, thought, feeling and conation.

Directly Freud clothed the elements of this harmony in the fabulous and emotional symbols of psychoanalysis, Freud invited schism. Jung and Adler have invented symbols which are at least as good explanations of the same phenomena, and yet they are totally opposed to each other and to Freud's in their significance. In Adler's fable the sexual 'instinct' makes hardly any appearance, yet his 'instinct of self-preservation' explains everything as satisfactorily as Freud's 'libido'. Since separate entities—such as an instinct of self-preservation or a Censor—are fabulous descriptions of certain innate physiological responses, it is not possible to find a crucial experiment to judge between Adler and Freud. They are disputing about myths, though the myths refer to real phenomena. In the same way Grecians might have disputed about inconsistencies in rival accounts of the birth of Athene from Zeus's head. What was actually being discussed by them was the modification of behaviour by experience or—more picturesquely—the Birth of Wisdom. Since both Athene and Zeus were mere symbolic fictions, such disputes about them were wasted time. Adler, Jung and Freud have wasted much of their time in precisely the same way.

Of them all Jung is perhaps the most scientific theoretically, even if he has made the fewer empirical discoveries, because he does realise the dualism inherent in Freud's approach. But he never escapes from that dualism. On the contrary, he makes it the foundation of his theories.

. . . . .

So far we have been concerned with psychology as shown by the organism's behaviour, and have neglected the environment except as simple stimulus. Restricting our study to the organism, we regard all psychic phenomena as simply certain patterns of innervations. Some of these innervations in ourselves are consciousness. As a whole they are part of a body's behaviour and we see part of this behaviour overtly as action, in ourselves or others. In the act of behaviour, the basic innervation patterns become modified. Thus the tune of a man's life begins with a simple hereditary phrase, on which experience plays endless variations, continually increasing in richness and subtlety. This is part of the fact that a man's life is lived in Reality, whose nature it is that each new present includes the previous past, so growing increasingly in complexity.

But all behaviour is interaction between body and stimuli from outside, or between one part of the body and another. The organism never behaves alone ; there is always an ' other ', the environment, which is a party to its behaviour. Moreover the environment too has its history, for it is subject to time. Thus it is never the same environment, and each transaction the organism has with it is subtly different because since the previous transaction it has become more full of history. Hence the behaviour of the organism is a counter-point, in which the organism furnishes one part and the environment the other part. We may for purposes of analysis consider the melody of each separately, but actually behaviour is not a melody but a harmony. Thus the harmony of the psyche is itself a reflection of the harmony of the body's being in reality. The treble of the consciousness is a reflection of the melody of the environment ; the bass of the unconsciousness is a reflection of the melody of the organism. The fundamental principle of physics is that each action has an equal and opposite reaction. Thus, after each act of behaviour, in which organism and environment interact, environment has affected organism and organism environment, and the resulting positions of each are different. Indeed that is why there is history, for the environment itself is simply a collection of mutually-interacting bodies. In between the act of an organism one moment and its act the next, the environment has changed, simply because the elements of which the environment is composed have interacted and changed each other.

Now of all known organisms, the human organism is the most elaborate in its melody and the most sensitive in its reaction to intercourse with reality. It is the organism which learns most from behaviour, from experience. Nothing changes so quickly as the human organism. In the same way the social environment, because the organisms of which it consists are chiefly human beings, also changes most quickly in between the acts of a human being. The study of this dialectic change is psychology from the point of view of the individual; but from the point of view of the sum of human beings it is sociology or history, and in its causal statement it must include all portions of the environment with which human beings interact, even the fixed stars. But since in the short periods usually studied, cosmical conditions do not change importantly, they may be neglected. They might become important in a study of humanity which included the Ice Ages. Of primary interest to history are however the material elements in the environment that do change rapidly in the periods generally studied, i.e. machines, transport, cities, and, in brief, all the social relations arising from social production, for the change in the organism will necessarily be related to these changing features in its environment. The organism does not enter consciously or of its own will into these relations. They are prior and determine its consciousness and will. It is in fact impossible to study psychology without a background of sociology. If one does do so, either it is impossible to find the causal connexion in the change of the human psyche, or else one accepts the human psyche as unchanging and all laws discovered from a study of contemporary psyches seem true for all time.

As it happens, no modern school of psychology has ever studied social relations as primary, as conditioning the consciousness which is generated by them. None study concrete society and its non-psychical basis. No modern school of psychology has ever yet got so far as to formulate its basic approach to the environment of the psyche it studies, continuous interaction with which is the law of psychic life.

Freud approaches his psychological problems with the assumptions of a bourgeois idealist, to whom nothing exists of reality save an unchanging backcloth before which the ideas play their parts. It is true that these ideas are now rather like the 'ruling passions' of older philosophers, and have been given the name of 'the instincts' or 'Libido', but the story is still the same fabulous drama, in which are performed the 'miracles' of inhibitions, sublimation, cathexis, narcissism, transformation and displacement, by those good and bad fairies, the censor, the ego, the super-ego and the id. There are even cannibal instincts and incest instincts, though it staggers the imagination of the biologist to infer how these variations evolved and became hereditary. There is no causality.

Freud imagines a pleasure-principle attempting to gain freedom for its pleasures within the bounds of the prison house of reality. Beyond those bounds of causality we must not stray, Freud admits, but inside their ever-contracting boundaries there appears to be true freedom. It is a fine fable. The instincts, like bourgeois revolutionaries, desperately attempt to gratify themselves, oppressed by the tyrant Reality's laws. Has such a conception any place in science?

Freud, like all bourgeois intellectuals, like Eddington, Russell and Wells, cannot lose his faith that there is a separate cell called liberty, mysteriously existing in the granite of scientific causality. Scientific thought is continually (it is supposed) contracting the dimensions of this chamber of little ease, but still it exists.

In particular, these thinkers suppose that man is more free, more at liberty, the more he is free from the pressure of culture, consciousness, and social organisation. Russell, Eddington, Freud, and Wells are alike in this supposition, which, carried (as they do not carry it) to the logical conclusion, means that the only beings with real liberty are the unconscious brutes.

But the truth is, the world is not a prison house of

reality in which man has been allotted by some miracle a honey cell of pleasure. Man is a part of reality, in constant relation with it, and the progress of consciousness, in so far as it increases his knowledge of causality, increases his freedom. In the same way, civilisation increases his freedom, in so far as it increases his causal control over reality, including himself. In this last, in the self-control of men as compared with their environmental control by machines, we are least advanced, and this is precisely because psychology, which would show us how to control ourselves, is always trying to evade causality. Science does not *seem* to be telling man about freedom. On the contrary, it seems only to be discovering cast-iron laws, of whose existence and rigidity he did not guess. But is an animal in a cage free because it does not realise it is a cage ? Will it not only become free when it realises that a locked cage completely restricts its movements and that to be free it must *necessarily* unlock the door ?

Bourgeois civilisation is built on this rock, that complete freedom consists in complete personal anarchy, and that man is *naturally* completely free. This Rousseaudism is found distorting all bourgeois thought. Freud cannot help visualising civilisation as the enslavement of the completely free instincts by culture.

Hence the honest bourgeois is always either pessimistic or religious. Man must have some conscious social organisation to exist socially (police, judges, factories, education), and all these seem to him so many limits to his freedom, not because of the *imperfection* of the organisation, which is the communist criticism, but because there is organisation at all. Thus to the bourgeois civilisation seems damned by its premises and there is no hope in this life of attaining freedom. All organisation, all consciousness, all thought eventually seem to the bourgeois intellectual the corruption or inhibition or repression of the completely free natural man ; but this natural man is an anthropoid ape, for man without society is a brute.

Can we talk of the inhibition or repression of that which is not free ? And are the instincts free or are they, as we see so clearly in the insect, blind mechanical enslavements, deaf to individual learning, heeding only the slow ancestral experience of the species ? Then society, creating by its 'inhibitions' and 'repressions' *consciousness*, is leading the instincts on the path not of slavery but of freedom. To call, as Freud does, that which frees the enslaved instincts 'inhibitions' or 'repression' is prejudiced.

Freud sees in the evolution of each individual psyche nothing but the drama of the instincts fighting among themselves, and so giving rise to the repressions of culture. He sees in culture nothing but the projection of this drama into the environment, on a collective scale : 'And now,' he says, 'it seems to me, the meaning of the evolution of culture is no longer a riddle to us. It must present to us the struggle between Eros and Death, between the instincts of life and the instincts of destruction, as it works itself out in the human species.' Thus to him culture is autonomously psychic, and without internal causality, just because it has no external connection. The material environment is ignored.

In another passage he attributes the organisations of society to the identifications of all individuals with each other through the father, thus explaining both social cohesion and leadership. And he adds (explaining our present discontents): 'This danger (i.e. social discontent) is most menacing where the social forces of cohesion consist predominantly of identifications of the individuals of the group with one another, whilst leading personalities fail to acquire the significance that should fall to them in the process of group-formation.' Here bourgeois idealism, long before the advent of Hitler, unwittingly writes the charter of barbarous Fascism, Fuhrership, and the Corporate State. Withdrawing from the future, Fascism appeals to a savage past for salvation. By a strange irony, Freud becomes the apologist of the Fascist philosophy which rejects him, which burns his books, and seems repugnant to him. Yet this is the irony of all bourgeois culture, that because it is based on a contradiction, it gives rise to the opposite of what it desires. It desires freedom and individual expression, but, because it believes freedom is to be found in abolition of social organisation, it gives rise to all the tyrannies and blind crippling necessities of the modern world. Freudism, attempting to cure civilisation of its instinctive distortions, points the way to Nazism.

Is Freud, then, an ally of Fascism, whose psychological mechanism in the individual his theory explains and condemns ? In one sense, yes ! As bourgeois consciousness breaks down before new reality, it is aware of its failure and this sense of failure is itself a disintegrating force. It is part of the rôle of Freud to make overt the rottenness in bourgeois social relations, but there are no 'absolutely hopeless' situations, and bourgeois culture defends itself from these humiliating awarenesses by the mechanism of barbaric pseudo-religious constructs, such as that of Fascist ideology. When consciousness reveals its inadequacy to a situation, one can either advance to a wider consciousness which will include the new situation that brought about the crisis, or one can regress to a former solution of a similar problem in the childhood of the individual or the nation. This is the mechanism of neuroses. But this is no solution, for the old situation is not the same situation, and the mind that faces it too has changed. So one gets only a false and pathological infantilism, full of illusion and phantasy. Freudism can point this out but, because of its lack of a scientific basis, it cannot show the way to attain the wider consciousness. Thus, after all, it is not a therapy, it is only a diagnosis. The analyst vainly exposes the regressive nature of the neurotic's solution, if he cannot himself provide a better solution. And Freud cannot. We can only cast out error with truth, and Freud had no new truth to offer, only a fairy-tale recording the breakdown of bourgeois civilisation as seen in its own mythological terms.

In answer to criticism of Freud's mythology, it has often been urged that Freudism is a therapy, not a science. Such defenders admit that emotively-charged concepts such as libido, the censor, the Œdipus complex and inhibition have no place in a scientific hypothesis. But (they argue) the neurosis is an emotional crisis, and the neurotic can only be cured emotionally. It is no use talking to him about conditioned reflexes. His emotions must be stirred, and this justifies the myths of psychoanalysis, by which truths are conveyed to him fabulously but vividly

But just because Freudism is not a science, it fails as a therapy. Granted that the neurotic must be touched emotionally, are individual psychoanalysts really arrogant enough to believe that the enormous, creative force of emotion, the dynamism of society, can be directed by them, as individuals, and by means of such arid concepts as those of Freudism? Emotion, in all its vivid colouring, is the creation of ages of culture acting on the blind unfeeling instincts. All art, all education, all day-to-day social experience, draw it out of the heart of the human genotype and direct and shape its myriad phenomena. Only society as a whole can really direct this force in the individual. To imagine that one psychoanalyst can shape it is to believe that one can bring down the houses of London with a shout. Could any discipline rooted in scientific causality have made so rash a misjudgment of the powers of the individual, as to believe that the mighty social force of emotion could be harnessed by 'Transference of libido ' to the earnest, middle-aged and bald physician? At least the Victorian heroine who wished to reform the sinner by a good woman's love had personal charm and unlimited opportunity.

The innate responses of an organism, the so-called instincts, as such are unconscious, mechanical, and unaffected by experience. Psychology therefore is not concerned with them, for they are the material of physiology. Psychology, in its study of consciousness or unconsciousness, can only have for its material all those psychic contents that results from the *modification* of responses by experience. It is this material that changes, that develops, that is distinctively human, that is of importance, and psychology should and in practice does ignore the *unchanging* instinctual basis as a cause. It concerns itself with the variable, which changes not only from age to age but from individual to individual and in an individual from hour to hour.

Reflexes are conditioned by experience, by action upon the environment. In man the environment consists of society, and action of education, daily work, daily life, what man sees, eats, hears, handles, travels in, co-operates in, loves, reverences, is repelled by—the whole fabric of social relations. These in the developing instinctual organism, produce the psyche, give consciousness its contents and the unconscious its trend, and make man what he is. Consciousness is the organ of social adaptation, but society is not composed of consciousnesses.

It is true that each contact of organism with the

environment not only affects the organism but also affects the environment. But in studying any one psyche, which is the task of individual psychology, we see on the one hand a naked genotype, dumb, ignorant and without tradition, whereas, on the other hand, forming its environment, we see not only millions of other individuals but the formulation in bricks and mortar, in social organisations, in religions, sciences, laws and language of the experience of æons of human activity. Consequently the action of the organism upon this mass of consciousness is minute compared with its reaction upon the organism, except in those cases where, owing to its own instability, the smallest touch is already sufficient to send it over violently into a new position. Such touches are administered by Marx. But in formulating a scientific psychology as in formulating a mechanics, the spectacular side is of no importance compared to the underlying causal laws, good for the ordinary as well as the exceptional event. The fact that in certain conditions of instability a cricket ball could cause the sun to explode, does not justify us in imagining that cricket balls exert forces greater than suns. In psychology, as in mechanics, the reaction of a body on its cosmic environment can be neglected, as compared to the effect of the world on the body.

Thus psychology must be extracted from sociology, not *vice versa*. For sociology, if scientific (and the only school of scientific sociology was founded by Marx), already includes the conscious formulations and the material accretions, arising from the dialectic of social relations, which provide the environment of the developing infant psyche. These are the social relations into which the organism enters irrespective of its will. The single organism is a slave to its environment, just as the particle is a slave to time and space, in spite of the fact that the social environment is composed of the activities of human organisms and time and space are the sum of the relations of particles. We must establish sociology before we can establish psychology, just as we must establish the laws of time and space before we can treat satisfactorily of a single particle. This is not to say that psychology and sociology are the same. Psychology has a province of tremendous importance to the human race, but it can only be studied scientifically on a background of more general laws, just as biology is impossible without the prior laws of physics and chemistry. Sociology is the foundation of psychology.

This Freud has failed to see. To him all mental phenomena are simply the interaction and mutual distortion of the instincts, of which culture and social organisations are a projection, and yet this social environment, produced by the instincts, is just what tortures and inhibits the instincts. Freud is powerless to explain causally the intricate and rich movement of cultural development, because he is in the position of a man trying to lift himself off the ground by his bootlaces. All this rich culture, its art, its science, and its institutions, is to Freud merely a projection of man's instinctive turmoil into unchanging reality, and yet this projection continually changes, although the individual instincts and reality remain the same. Why do social relations change? Why do psyches alter from age to age? Freud, like all modern psychologists who base themselves on the unchanging instincts of the genotype, is powerless to explain the only thing that interests psychology, the thing that *constitutes* psychology, the perpetual variation and development of the mental phenotype. Like Plato's men in the cave, psychoanalysts try to deduce from shadows what is happening outside. Looking into the psyche, they are mystified by the movements caused by currents in outer reality and mistake them for the distortions of the cunning and oppressed instincts, or for the interventions of mysterious 'forces' that are generated by the instincts. Seeing the shadows make a circular détour round one place, they assume this to be an eternal law of the psyche, the Œdipus complex. It does not occur to them that it may be due to an obstacle in the environment, round which the shadows have to move, and that the complex will alter if the obstacle is moved.

Unable to see psychology causally simply because they cannot see it sociologically, Freudism can attain to no psychology beyond bourgeois psychology. They never advance beyond the view-point of the 'individual in civil society'. Whether they study primitive man or lay down general laws of the soul, it is always with ideas formulated from a bourgeois psyche studying other bourgeois psyches, and so the instincts play always the part of splendid and free brutes, crippled by the repressions of a cruel culture. It is true that to-day the system of production relations is crippling man's splendid powers, but Freudian 'libido' in bondage to 'repression' is a very inadequate myth to convey this reality. It is a pale subjective reflection of the vital objective situation. The old bourgeois symbol of 'original sin' is better. The psyche, a creation of its environment, becomes to Freud, who ignores the environment or is ignorant of its mode of change, a creature whom mysterious self-generated entities force to become an unhappy bourgeois psyche. It is as if a man, seeing a row of trees bent in various ways by the prevailing winds, were without studying the relation between growth and environment to deduce that a mysterious complex in trees caused them always to lean as the result of a death instinct attracting them to the ground, while eternal Eros bade them spring up vertically. Freud's error is so much the worse because the psyche, studied by psychology, is far more the result of environmental conditions than the whole tree. The psyche is the organ of adaptation to social relations, therefore for psychology the laws determining social relations are fundamental.

Thus Freudism, like all 'individual' psychologies, breaks down in the most elementary scientific desideratum, that of causality. Though evolved as a therapy, it turns out to be the creed of undiluted pessimism.

If we do not know the laws of our environment, we cannot know ourselves, and if we cannot know ourselves, we can never be free. If we are full of bitterness, and this bitterness is the outcome of an inevitable instinctual strife, our hearts can never be sweetened. If we owe no vital part of our consciousness to our environment, it is of no value to change it. 'New skies,' said Horace, 'the exile finds, but the same heart.'—If we regard the categories of the present as final, and the present is full of despair and neurosis, of slumps and wars, we can never pass beyond them to a successful issue. At the best, like the neurotic, we can only return to a former successful solution at an infantile level—to feudalism, barbarian group-leadership, *unanisme*, Fascism. Indeed Jung invokes as our only salvation this very regression, appealing to the old barbarous mythologies to come to our aid. Freud at least has the courage to spurn this way of escape, and so, like a Roman stoic, in decaying classical civilisation he treads the die-hard path, and drinks the cup of poison to its dregs.

This conception, apparently refined, of the last fatal battle of the gods, is really barbarous, and the first step in the path to Hindoo resignation and vegetable sanctity. Spengler is the prophet of this resignation to one's own limitations :

'Only dreamers believe that there is a way out. We are born in this time and must bravely follow the path to the destined end. There is no other way. Our duty is to hold on to the last position, without hope, without rescue.' Freud, too, in *The Future of an Illusion* and *Group Psychology*, sees little hope for culture. Yet he is, in spite of this, more optimistic than the Communist in that he believes that while society rushes downhill, the psychoanalyst, as an individual, can do what all society fails to do, and cure the neurotic produced by modern conditions. This contradictory belief that the individual can do what the sum of individuals, of which he is one, cannot do, is characteristic of all these bourgeois pessimists, and makes it difficult to take their pessimism as completely sincere.

It is generally believed that the relation between environment and individual is correctly expressed in Adler, exponent of Individual psychology, and Freud's former pupil. Let us therefore hear him :

> 'In a civilisation where one man is the enemy of the other—for this is what our whole industrial system means—demoralisation is ineradicable, for demoralisation and crime are the by-products of the struggle for existence as known to our industrialised civilisation.'

Surely, it will be said, Adler has escaped from the bourgeois cage. Surely he has realised that it is the environment, bourgeois capitalism, that produces our present discontents, and not the struggle-for-existence of the organism, pushed on by its instincts, that produces bourgeois capitalism. True, he here confuses industrialisation (machine technique) with the competition of capitalism which gave rise to it, but is separable from it. He is confounding productive forces and productive relations. Yet, at least (it will be urged), the root of the matter is in him. Let us therefore continue the quotation and see his remedy for this 'ineradicable' demoralisation: 'To limit and do away with this demoralisation, a chair of curative pedagogy should be established.'

This is the logic of Individual Psychology! Man's demoralisation, his neurosis, his discontent, his despair, are correctly seen to be due to his environment—capitalist social relations. To cure it, however, his environment is not to be changed, for the environment is always in all bourgeois economics and sociology and in spite of history presumed to be unchangeable. Rather, man is to lift himself off the ground by his bootlaces; to take pedagogic pills to cure the earthquake of capitalism's collapse. The pill takes various forms: It is a chair of curative pedagogy with Adler. With Freud the sufferers, if rich enough, are to go to an analyst for a course of treatment. This is impracticable, Jung realises, for the poorer classes, so we must re-introduce the old myths, of the archetypal hero swallowed by the giant fish ('Psychology of the Unconscious'.) These are the doctors who stand by the bedside of society in its most gigantic agony! Is it surprising that the criticism of the Marxist sometimes contains a tinge of contempt?

The Marxian has been often reproached for his antagonism to psychoanalysis. It is even asserted that the founder, it is said, has no bourgeois illusions; he is a thoroughgoing materialist. But he is not. Freud is still possessed by the focal bourgeois illusion, that the individual stands opposed to an unchanging society which trammels him, and within whose constraints his instincts attempt freely to develop the rich and varied phenomena of the psyche. Because of that illusion Freud thinks society itself is doomed to frustration, and yet thinks that one individual can cure another. He is never able to see that just as man must have a fulcrum outside him to lift himself, so the individual must act on the environment which created his consciousness in order to change it. We owe much to Freud for his symbolic presentation of the discord between the deep and recent layers of men's minds ; but he cannot heal us, for he cannot even teach us that first truth, that we must change the world in order to change ourselves.

The revolt of all the instincts against current social relations, which to Freud is everything and obscures his whole horizon, so that he writes all psychology, art, religion, culture, politics and history in terms of this revolt, is only one of many signals to the Marxian that, behind the decayed façade, a new environment is being realised and in man's troubled soul a wider consciousness, too, awaits delivery.

VIII

LIBERTY

A STUDY IN BOURGEOIS ILLUSION

MANY will have heard a broadcast by H. G. Wells in which (commenting on the Soviet Union) he described it as a 'great experiment which has but half fulfilled its promise', it is still a 'land without mental freedom'. There are also many essays of Bertrand Russell in which this philosopher explains the importance of liberty, how the enjoyment of liberty is the highest and most important goal of man. Fisher claims that the history of Europe during the last two or three centuries is simply the struggle for liberty. Continually and variously by artists, scientists, and philosophers alike, liberty is thus praised and man's right to enjoy it imperiously asserted.

I agree with this. Liberty does seem to me the most important of all generalised goods—such as justice, beauty, truth—that come so easily to our lips. And yet when freedom is discussed a strange thing is to be noticed. These men—artists, careful of words, scientists, investigators of the entities denoted by words, philosophers, scrupulous about the relations between words and entities—never define precisely what they mean by freedom. They seem to assume that it is quite a clear concept, whose definition everyone would agree about.

Yet who does not know that liberty is a concept about whose nature men have quarrelled perhaps more than about any other? The historic disputes concerning predestination, Karma, Free-Will, Moira, salvation by faith or works, determinism, Fate, Kismet, the categorical imperative, sufficient grace, occasionalism, Divine Providence, punishment and responsibility have all been about the nature of man's freedom of will and action. The Greeks, the Romans, the Buddhists, the Mahomedans, the Catholics, the Jansenists, and the Calvinists, have each had different ideas of liberty. Why, then, do all these bourgeois intellectuals assume that liberty is a clear concept, understood in the same way by all their hearers, and therefore needing no definition? Russell, for example, has spent his life finding a really satisfactory definition of number and even now it is disputed whether he has been successful. I can find in his writings no clear definition of what he means by liberty. Yet most people would have supposed that men are far more in agreement as to what is meant by a number, than what is meant by liberty.

This indefinite use of the words can only mean either that they believe the meaning of the word invariant in history or that they use it in the contemporary bourgeois sense. If they believe the meaning invariant, it is strange that men have disputed so often about freedom. These intellectuals must surely be incapable of such a blunder. They must mean liberty as men in their situation experience it. That is, they must mean by liberty to have no more restrictions imposed on them than they endure at that time. They do not—these Oxford dons or successful writers—want, for example, the restrictions of Fascism, that is quite clear. That would not be liberty. But at present, thank God, they are reasonably free.

Now this conception of liberty is superficial, for not all their countrymen are in the same situation. A, an intellectual with a good education, in possession of a modest income, with not too uncongenial friends, unable to afford a yacht, which he would like, but at least able to go to the winter sports, considers this (more or less) freedom. He would like that yacht, but still—he can write against communism or Fascism or the existing system. Let us for the moment grant that A is free. I propose to analyse this statement more deeply in a moment, and show that it is partial. But let us for the moment grant that A enjoys liberty.

Is B free ? B is the sweated non-union shop-assistant of Houndsditch, working seven days of the week. He knows nothing of art, science, or philosophy. He has no culture except a few absurd prejudices, his elementary school education saw to that. He believes in the superiority of the English race, the King's wisdom and loving-kindness to his subjects, the real existence of God, the Devil, Hell, and Sin, and the wickedness of sexual intercourse unless palliated by marriage. His knowledge of world events is derived from the *News of the World*, on other days he has no time to read the papers. He believes that when he dies he will (with luck) enter into eternal bliss. At present, however, his greatest dread is that, by displeasing his employer in some trifle, he may become unemployed.

B's trouble is plainly lack of leisure in which to cultivate freedom. C does not suffer from this. He is an unemployed middle-aged man. He is free for 24 hours a day. He is free to go anywhere—in the streets and parks, and in the Museums. He is allowed to think of anything—the Einstein theory, the Frege definition of classes, or the doctrine of the Immaculate Conception. Regrettably enough, he does none of these things. He quarrels with his wife, who calls him a good-for-nothing waster, and with his children, who because of the Means Test have to pay his rent, and with his former friends, because they can enjoy pleasures he cannot afford. Fortunately he is free to remove himself from existence, and this one afternoon, when his wife is out and there is plenty of money in the gas-meter, he will do.

A is free. Are B and C? I assume that A will reply that B and C are not free. If A asserts that B and C do enjoy real liberty, most of us, without further definition, will know what to think of A's idea of liberty. But a Wells, a Forster, or a Russell would doubtless agree, as vehemently as us, that this is not liberty, but a degrading slavery to environment. He will say that to free B and C we must raise them to A's level, the level, let us say, of the Oxford don. Like the Oxford don, B and C must have leisure and a modest income with which to enjoy the good things and the good ideas of the world.

But how is this to be brought about? Bourgeois social relations are what we have now. No one denies that the dynamic motive of such relations is private profit. Here bourgeois economists and Marxists are agreed. Moreover, if causality has any meaning, and unless we are to throw all scientific method overboard, current economic relations and the unfreedom of B and C must be causally inter-related.

We have, then, bourgeois social relations on the one hand, and these varying degrees of unfreedom—A, B, and C—on the other hand, interconnected as cause and effect. So far, either might be cause, for we have not yet decided whether mental states arise from social relations, or *vice versa*. But as soon as we ask how action is to solve the problem, we see which is primary. It is useless to give B, by means of lectures and picture galleries, opportunity for understanding philosophy or viewing masterpieces of art. He has no time to acquire, before starting work, the taste for them or after starting work the time to gratify it. Nor is C free to enjoy the riches of bourgeois culture as long as his whole existence is clouded by his economic position. It is circumstances that are imprisoning consciousness, not *vice versa*. It is not because B and C are unenlightened that they are members of the working class, but because they are members of the working class, they are unenlightened. And Russell, who writes *In Praise of Idleness*, praises rightly, for he is clever because he is idle and bourgeois, not idle and bourgeois because he is clever.

We now see the cause and effect of the situation. We see that it is not this freedom and unfreedom which produce bourgeois social relations, but that bourgeois social relations alike give rise to these two extremes, the freedom of the idle bourgeois, and the unfreedom of the proletarian worker. It is plain that this effect, if undesirable, can only be changed by changing the cause.

Thus the intellectual is faced with another problem, like that when he had to define more precisely who enjoyed the liberty he regarded as contemporary. Does he wish that there should exist for ever these two states of captivity and freedom, of misery and happiness ? Can he enjoy a freedom which is sustained by the same cause as the workers' unfreedom ? For if not, he must advance further, and say, 'bourgeois social relations must be changed'. Change they will, precisely because of this unfreedom they increasingly generate ; but to-day the intellectual must decide whether his will will be part of the social forces making for change, or vainly pitted against them.

But how are bourgeois social relations to be changed ? Not by a mere effort of the will, for we saw that the mind was made by social relations, not *vice versa.* It is matter, the quantitative foundation of qualitative ideology, that must be changed. It is not enough to argue and convince. Work must be done. The environment must be altered.

Science shows us how. We achieve our wants always, not by the will alone, not by merely wishing them into being, but with action aided by cognition, by utilising the physical laws of reality. We move mountains, not by the mere movement of desire, but because we understand the rigidly determined laws of kinetics, hydraulics, and electrical engineering and can guide our actions by them. We attain freedom—that is, the fulfilment of our will—by obedience to the laws of reality. Observance of these laws is simple; it is the discovery of them that is the difficulty, and this is the task of science.

Thus, the task of defining liberty becomes still harder. It is not so easy after all to establish even a contemporary definition of liberty. Not only has the intellectual already had to decide to change bourgeois social relations, but he must now find out the laws of motion of society, and fit social relations into a causal scheme. It is not enough to want to be free; it is also necessary to know.

Only one scientific analysis of the law of motion of social relations exists, that of Marxism. For the understanding of how, physically, at the material level of social being, quantitative movements of capital, of matter, of *stuff*, provide the causal predictive basis of society, and pass via social relations into the qualitative changes of mind, will, and ideology, it is necessary to refer the bourgeois intellectual to Marx, Engels, Plekhanov, Lenin and Bukharin. Let us suppose that he has now done this and returns again to the difficult pursuit of liberty.

His causal conception of society will now enable him to realise that the task of making social relations produce liberty is as rigidly conditioned by reality as the task of making matter fulfil his desire in the form of machines. All matter—machinery, capital, men—and the relations which they exhibit in society—can only move in accordance with causal laws. This involves first that the old relations must be broken down, just as a house must be pulled down if we would entirely rebuild it, and the transition, pulling up and putting down, must follow certain laws. We cannot pull up the foundation first, or build the roof before the walls.

This transitional stage involves the alteration of all the adherences between humans and the capital, machinery and materials, which mediate social relations. These must no longer adhere to individual persons—the bourgeois class—but to all members of society. This change is not a mere change of ownership, for it also involves that no individuals can derive profit from ownership without working. The goods are not destined to go the round of the market—the profit movement—but directly into use—the use movement. Moreover, this involves that all the visible institutions depending on private profit relations—laws, church, bureaucracy, judiciary, army, police, education—must be pulled down and rebuilt. The *bourgeoisie* cannot do this, for it is by means of these very institutions—private property (the modest income), law, university, civil service, privileged position, etc.—

that they attain their freedom. To expect them to destroy these relations on which, as we saw, their freedom, and the workers' unfreedom, depend, is to ask them to go in quest of captivity, which, since liberty is what all men seek, they will not do. But the opposite is the case with the unfree, with the proletariat. The day they go in search of liberty, they revolt. The bourgeois, fighting for his liberty, must necessarily find himself in antagonism to the non-bourgeois, also fighting for liberty. The eventual issue of this struggle is due to the fact that capitalist economy, as it develops, makes ever narrower the class which really owns liberty, until the day comes when the intellectual, the doctor, the petty bourgeois, the clerk, and the peasant, realise that they too are not after all free. And they see that the fight of the proletariat is their fight.

What, to the proletarian, is liberty—the extermination of those bourgeois institutions and relations which hold them in captivity—is necessarily compulsion and restraint to the bourgeois, just as the old bourgeois liberty generated non-liberty for the worker. The two notions of liberty are irreconcilable. Once the proletariat is in power, all attempts to re-establish bourgeois social relations will be attacks on proletarian liberty, and will therefore be repulsed as fiercely as men repulse all attacks on their liberty. This is the meaning of the dictatorship of the proletariat, and why with it there is censorship, ideological acerbity, and all the other devices developed by the bourgeois in the evolution of the coercive State which secures his freedom.

There is, however, one vital difference. Bourgeois social relations, generating the liberty of the bourgeois and the non-liberty of the proletarian, depend on the existence of both freedom and unfreedom for their continuance. The bourgeois could not enjoy his idleness without the labour of the worker, nor the worker remain in a bourgeois relationship without the coercive guidance and leadership of the bourgeois. Thus the liberty of the few is, in bourgeois social relations, built on the unfreedom of the many. The two Nations dwell in perpetual antagonism. But after the dispossession of the bourgeoisie, the antagonism between the expropriated and therefore unfree bourgeois, and the inheriting and therefore free proletariat, is only temporary. For the owners of the means of production, being also the workers of that means, do not need the existence of an expropriated class. When, therefore, the transition is complete, and the bourgeois class is either absorbed or has died out, there is no longer an unfree compelled class. That is what is meant by the 'withering away' of the State into a classless society, after the transitional period such as is now taking place in Russia.

This, stated in its simplest terms, is the causal process whereby bourgeois social relations can change into new social relations not generating a mass of unfreedom as the opposite pole to a little freedom. We have purposely made it simple. A fuller discussion, such as

Marx gives, would make clearer the fluid interpenetrating nature of the process ; how it is brought about causally by capitalist economy itself, which cannot stand still, but clumps continually into greater centralisation, giving rise to imperialistic wars, which man will not forever tolerate, and to viler and viler cash relations, filling men with hate, which will one day become hate for the system. And as capitalism perpetrates these enormities, the cause of revolt, it gives the proletariat the means of revolt, by making them unite, become more conscious and organised, so that, when the time of revolt comes, they have both the solidarity and executive ability needed to take over the administration of the bourgeois property. At the same time bourgeois social relations reveal that even their freedom is not real freedom, that bourgeois freedom is almost as imprisoning to its enjoyers as the worker's unfreedom. And thus the *bourgeoisie* does not find itself as a solid class, arrayed against the proletariat, but there are divisions in its own ranks, a few at first, and then more and more. The revolution takes place as soon as the proletariat are sufficiently organised by their fight against bourgeois social relations to co-operate, sufficiently harried by their growing unfreedom to demand a new world at all costs ; and when, on the other side, as a result of the developing contradictions of capitalism, the bourgeois themselves have lost their grip.

Let us, therefore, go deeper, and examine more closely the true nature of bourgeois freedom. Are

H. G. Wells, Bertrand Russell, E. M. Forster, you, reader, and I, really free ? Do we enjoy even mental freedom ? For if we do not enjoy that, we certainly do not enjoy physical freedom.

Bertrand Russell is a philosopher and a mathematician. He takes the method of science seriously, and applies it to various fields of thought. He believes that thoughts are simply special arrangements of matter, even though he calls matter mind-stuff. He agrees that to every psychism corresponds a neurism, that life is a special chemical phenomenon, just as thought is a special biological phenomenon. He is not taken in by the nonsense of entelechies and pure memory.

Why then does he refrain from applying these categories, used everywhere else, to the concept of liberty ? In what sense can he believe man to be ever completely free ? What meaning can he attach to the word freedom ? He rightly detects the idealistic hocus-pocus of smuggling God into science as the Life-Force, entelechy, or the first cause, for the sleight of hand it is. But his liberty is a kind of God ; something which he accepts on faith, somehow intervening in the affairs of the universe, and unconnected with causality. Russell's liberty and his philosophy live in different worlds. He has made theology meet science, and seen that theology is a barbarous relic. But he has not performed the last act of integration ; he has not asked science's opinion of this belief that the graduate of one of the better universities, with a moderate income, considerable intelligence, and some leisure, is really free.

It is not a question of whether man has in some mysterious fashion free will. For if that were the problem, all men either would or would not have free will, and therefore all men would or would not have liberty. If freedom consists in having free will, and men have free will, we can will as freely under a Fascist, or proletarian, as under a bourgeois Government. But everyone admits that there are degrees of liberty. In what therefore does this difference in liberty consist?

Although liberty does not then depend on free will, it will help us to understand liberty if we consider what is the freedom of the will. Free will consists in this, that man is conscious of the motive that dictates his action. Without this consciousness of antecedent motive, there is no free will. I raise my hand to ward off a blow. The blow dictated my action; none the less, I was conscious that I wanted to ward off the blow; I willed to do so. My will was free; it was an act of my will. There was a cause; but I was conscious of a free volition. And I was conscious of the cause, of the blow.

In sleep a tickling of the soles of the feet actuates the plantar reflex. Such an action we call involuntary. Just as the warding movement was elicited by an outside stimulus, so was the bending of the leg. None the less, we regard the second as unfree, *in*voluntary. It was not preceded by a conscious motive. Nor were we conscious of the cause of our action. We thus see that free will exists in so far as we are conscious of an antecedent motive in our mind, regarded as the immediate cause of action. If this motive, or act of will, is itself free, and not forced, we must also be in turn conscious of the antecedent motive that produced it. Free will is not therefore the opposite of causality ; it is on the contrary a special and late aspect of causality, it is the *consciousness* of causality. That is why man naturally fits all happenings outside him in a causal frame ; because he is conscious of causality in himself. Otherwise it would be a mystery if man, experiencing only uncausality in free will, should assume, as he does, that all other things are linked by causality. If, however, he is only assuming that other objects obey the same laws as he does, both the genesis and success of causality as a cognitive framework for reality are explicable.

Causality and freedom thus are aspects of each other. Freedom is the consciousness of necessity. The universe as a whole is completely free, because that which is not free is determined by something else outside it. But all things are, by definition, contained in the universe, therefore the universe is determined by nothing but itself. But every individual thing in the universe is determined by other things, because the universe is material. This materiality is not 'given' in the definition of the universe, but is exactly what science establishes when it explains the world actively and positively.

Thus the only absolute freedom, like the only absolute truth, is the universe itself. But parts of the universe have varying degrees of freedom, according to their degrees of self-determination. In self-determination, the causes are within the thing itself ; thus, in the sensation of free will, the antecedent cause of an action is the conscious thought of an individual, and since the action is also that of the individual, we talk of freedom, because there is self-determination.

The freedom of free will can only be relative. It is characteristic of the more recently evolved categories that they contain more freedom. The matter of which man is composed is in spatio-temporal relation with all other matter in the universe, and its position in space and time is only to a small degree self-determined. Man's perception, however, is to a less degree in relation with the rest of the universe ; it is a more exclusive kind of perception that sees little not in the immediate vicinity of man, or in which it is not interested, and it is largely moulded by memory, that is, by internal causes. Hence it is freer, more self-determined, than the spatio-temporal relations of dead matter. Man's consciousness is still more self-determined, particularly in its later developments, such as conscious volition.

Man constantly supposes that he is freer than he is. Freudian research has recently shown that events at the level of being—i.e. unconscious physiological events—may give rise to disturbances which usurp conscious functions. In such circumstances a man may not be conscious of the motives of his actions, although he believes he is. He is therefore unfree, for his will's determination arises from events outside consciousness. An example is the neurotic. The neurotic is unfree. He attains freedom by attaining self-determination, that is, by making conscious, motives which before were unconscious. Thus he becomes captain of his soul. I am not now discussing the validity of the various methods by which this knowledge is obtained, or what neurological meaning we are to give to the Freudian symbolism. I agree with this basic assumption of Freudian thereapy, that man always obtains more freedom, more self-determination, by a widening of consciousness or, in other words, by an increase of knowledge. In the case of his own mind, man, by obtaining a knowledge of its causality, and the necessity of its functioning, obtains more freedom. Here too freedom is seen to be a special form of determinism, namely, the consciousness of it.

But man cannot simply sit and contemplate his own mind in order to grasp its causality. His body, and likewise his mind, is in constant metabolic relation with the rest of the universe. As a result, when we want to trace any causal mental sequence, in order to be conscious of it, we find it inextricably commingled with events in the outer world. At an early stage we find we must seek freedom in the outer as well as the inner world. We must be conscious, not only of our own laws, but of those of outer reality. Man has always realised that whatever free will may mean it is not will alone, but action also which is involved in liberty. For example, I am immersed in a plaster cast so that I cannot blink an eyelid. None the less, my will is completely free. Am I therefore completely free? Only extremely idealistic philosophers would suggest that I am. A free will is therefore not enough to secure liberty, but our actions also must be unconstrained. Now everyone realises that the outer environment continually constrains our freedom, and that free will is no freedom unless it can act what it wills. It follows that to be really free we must also be able to do what we freely will to do.

But this freedom, too, leads us back to determinism. For we find, and here no philosopher has ever disputed it, that the environment is completely deterministic. That is to say, whatever motion or phenomenon we see, there is always a cause for it, which is itself caused, and so on. And the same causes, in the same circumstances, always secure the same effects. Now an understanding of this iron determinism brings freedom. For the more we understand the causality of the universe, the more we are able to do what we freely will. Our knowledge of the causality of water enables us to build ships and cross the seas; our knowledge of the laws of air enables us to fly; our knowledge of the inevitable behaviour of materials enables us to build houses and bridges; our knowledge of the necessary movements of the planets enables us to construct calendars so that we sow, embark on voyages, and set out to meet each other at the times most conducive to achieving what we will to do. Thus, in the outer world too, determinism is seen to produce freedom, freedom is understood to be a special form of necessity, the *consciousness* of necessity. We see that we attain freedom by our consciousness of the causality of subjective mental phenomena together with our consciousness of the causality of external phenomena. And we are not surprised that the characteristic of the behaviour of objects—causality—is also a characteristic of consciousness, for consciousness itself is only an aspect of an object—the body. The more we gain of this double understanding, the more free we become, possessing both free will and free action. These are not two mutually exclusive things, free will versus determinism—but on the contrary they play into each other's hands.

From this it follows that the animals are less free than men. Creatures of impulse, acting they know not why, subject to all the chances of nature, of other animals, of geographical accidents and climatic change, they are at the mercy of necessity, precisely because they are unconscious of it.

That is not to say they have no freedom, for they possess a degree of freedom. They have some knowledge of the causality of their environment, as is shown by their manipulations of time and space and material—the bird's flight, the hare's leap, the ant's nest. They have some inner self-determination, as is shown by their behaviour. But compared to man, they are unfree.

Implicit in the conception of thinkers like Russell and Forster, that all social relations are restraints on spontaneous liberty, is the assumption that the animal is the only completely free creature. No one constrains the solitary carnivore to do anything. This is of course an ancient fallacy. Rousseau is the famous exponent. Man is born free but is everywhere in chains. Always in the bourgeois mind is this legend of a golden age, of a perfectly good man corrupted by institutions. Unfortunately not only is man not good without institutions, he is not evil either. He is no man at all ; he is neither good nor evil ; he is an unconscious brute.

Russell's idea of liberty is the unphilosophical idea of bestiality. Narkover School is not such a bad illustration of Russell's liberty after all. The man alone, unconstrained, answerable only to his instincts, is Russell's free man. Thus all man's painful progress from the beasts is held to be useless. All men's work and sweat and revolutions have been away from freedom. If this is true, and if a man believes, as most of us do, as Russell does, that freedom is the essential goal of human effort, then civilisation should be abandoned and we should return to the woods. I am a Communist because I believe in freedom. I criticise Russell, and Wells, and E. M. Forster, because I believe they are the champions of unfreedom.

But this is going too far, it will be said. How can these men, who have defended freedom of thought, action, and morality, be champions of unfreedom ? Let us proceed with our analysis and we shall see why.

Society is a creation by which man attains a fuller measure of freedom than the beasts. It is society and society alone, that differentiates man qualitatively from the beasts. The essential feature of society is economic production. Man, the individual, cannot do what he wants alone. He is unfree alone. Therefore he attains freedom by co-operation with his fellows. Science, by which he becomes conscious of outer reality, is social. Art, by which he becomes conscious of his feelings, is social. Economic production, by which he makes outer reality conform to his feeling, is social, and generates in its interstices science and art. It is economic production then that gives man freedom. It is because of economic production that man is free, and beasts are not. This is clear from the fact that economic production is the manipulation, by means of agriculture, horse-taming, road-building, car-construction, light, heating, and other engineering, of the environment, conformably to man's will. It enables man to do what he wills ; and he can only do what he wills with the help of others. Without roads, food supplies, machines, houses, and clothes, he would be like the man in a plaster cast, who can will what he likes, and yet is not a free man but a captive. But even his free will depends on it. For consciousness develops by the evolution of language, science, and art, and these are all born of economic production. Thus the freedom of man's actions depends on his material level, on his economic production. The more advanced the economic production, the freer the civilisation.

But, it will be argued, economic production is just what entails all the ' constraints ' of society. Daily work, division of labour under superintendents, all the laws of contract and capital, all the regulations of society, arise out of this work of economic production. Precisely, for, as we saw, freedom is the consciousness of causality. And by economic production, which makes it possible for man to achieve in action his will, man becomes conscious of the means *necessary* to achieve it. That a lever *must* be of a certain length to move the stone man *wills* to move is one consequence ; the other is that a certain number of men *must* co-operate in a certain way to wield the lever. From this it is only a matter of development to the complicated machinery of modern life, with all its elaborate social relations.

Thus all the ' constraints ', ' obligations ', ' inhibitions ', and ' duties ' of society are the very means by which freedom is obtained by men. Liberty is thus the social consciousness of necessity. Liberty is not just necessity, for all reality is united by necessity. Liberty is the consciousness of necessity—in outer reality, in myself, and in the social relations which mediate between outer reality and human selves. The beast is a victim of mere necessity, man is in society conscious and self-determined. Not of course absolutely so, but more so than the beast.

Thus freedom of action, freedom to do what we will, the vital part of liberty, is seen to be secured by the social consciousness of necessity, and to be generated in the process of economic production. The price of liberty is not eternal vigilance, but eternal work.

But what is the relation of society to the other part of liberty, freedom to will ? Economic production makes man free to do what he wills, but is he free to will what he will ?

We saw that he was only free to do what he willed by attaining the consciousness of outer necessity. It is equally true that he is only free to will what he will by attaining the consciousness of inner necessity. Moreover, these two are not antagonistic, but, as we shall now find, they are one. Consciousness is the result of a specific and highly important form of economic production.

Suppose someone had performed the regrettable experiment of turning Bertrand Russell, at the age of nine months, over to a goat foster-mother, and leaving him to her care, in some remote spot, unvisited by human beings, to grow to manhood. When, say forty years later, men first visited Bertrand Russell, would they find him with the manuscripts of the *Analysis of Mind* and the *Analysis of Matter* in his hands? Would they even find him in possession of his definition of number, as the class of all classes? No. In contradiction to his present state, his behaviour would be both illogical and impolite.

It looks, therefore, as if Russell, as we know and value him, is primarily a social product. Russell is a philosopher and not an animal because he was taught not only manners, but language, and so given access to the social wisdom of ages of effort. Language filled his head with ideas, showed him what to observe, taught him logic, put all other men's wisdom at his disposal, and awoke in him affectively the elementary decencies of society—morality, justice, and liberty. Russell's consciousness, like that of all useful social objects, was a creation. It is Russell's consciousness that is distinctively him, that is what we value in him, as compared to an anthropoid ape. Society made him, just as it makes a hat.

It goes without saying that Russell's 'natural gifts' (or, as we say more strictly, his genotype) were of importance to the outcome. But that is only to say that the material conditions the finished product. Society is well aware that it cannot make a silk purse out of a sow's ear or, except in special circumstances, a don out of a cretin. But it is also aware that out of iron ore you can make rocks, bridges, ships, or micrometers, and, out of that plastic material, man's genotype, you can make Aztecs, ancient Egyptians, Athenians, Prussians, proletarians, parsons, or public schoolboys.

It also goes almost without saying that a man is not a hat. He is a unique social product, the original of Butler's fantasy of machines that gave birth to machines. He himself is one of those machines. The essential truth about man, as compared with hats, is that he is not a hat, but the man who wears it. And the essential truth about this fashioning process of man by society, is that the fashioning is primarily of his consciousness, a process that does not take place with anything else. Now it is precisely because society elaborates his consciousness, that man, although a social product like a hat, is capable of free will, whereas a hat, being unconscious, is not capable of free will. The coming-to-be of a man, his 'growing up', is society fashioning *itself*, a group of consciousnesses, themselves made by previous consciousnesses, making another. So the torch of liberty is handed on, and burns still brighter. But it is in living that man's consciousness takes its distinctive stamp, and living is simply entering into social relations.

But, it will be urged, man—the individual—sees the world for himself alone—mountains, sky, and sea. Alone in his study he reflects on fate and death. True. But mountains and sea have a meaning to him, precisely because he is articulate-speaking, because he has a socially-moulded consciousness. Death, fate, and sea are highly-evolved social concepts. Each individual contributes a little to altering and elaborating them, but how small a contribution compared to the immense pressure of the past! Language, science, and art are all simply the results of man's uniting with his fellows socially to learn about himself and outer reality, in order to impose his desires upon it. Both knowledge and effort are only possible in co-operation, and both are made necessary by man's struggles to be freer.

Thus man's inner freedom, the conscious will, acting towards conscious ends, is a product of society; it is an economic product. It is the most refined of the products society achieves in its search for freedom. Social consciousness flowers out of social effort. We give vent in effort to our instinctive desires. Learning how to accomplish them, we learn something about the nature of reality and how to master it. This wisdom modifies the nature of our desires, which become more conscious, more full of accurate images of reality. So enriched, the desires become subtler, and, in working to achieve profounder goals, in more elaborate economic production, gain still deeper insight into reality, and, as consequence, themselves become yet more enriched. Thus, in dialectic process, social being generates social mind, and this interplay between deepening inner and outer reality is conserved and passed on by culture. Man, as society advances, has a consciousness composed less and less of unmodified instinct, more and more of socially-fashioned knowledge and emotion. Man understands more and more clearly the necessities of his own being and of outer reality. He becomes increasingly more free.

The illusion that our minds are free to the extent that, like the beasts, we are unconscious of the causality of our mental states, is just what secures our unfreedom. Bourgeois society to-day clearly exhibits in practice this truth, which we have established by analysis in theory. The bourgeois believes that liberty consists in absence of social organisation ; that liberty is a negative quality, a deprivation of existing obstacles to it ; and not a positive quality, the reward of endeavour and wisdom. This belief is itself the outcome of bourgeois social relations. As a result of it, the bourgeois intellectual is unconscious of the causality that makes his consciousness what it is. Like the neurotic who refuses to believe that his compulsion is the result of a certain unconscious complex, the bourgeois refuses to believe that his conception of liberty as a mere deprivation of social restraints arises from bourgeois social relations themselves, and that it is just this illusion which is constraining him on every side. He refuses to see that his own limited liberty ; the captivity of the worker, and all the contradictions of developing bourgeois relations —pacifism, fascism, war, hate, cruelty, disease—are bound in one net of causality, that each is influenced by each, and that therefore it is fallacious to suppose a simple effort of the will of the free man, without knowledge of the causes, will banish fascism, war, and slumps. Because of his basic fallacy, this type of intellectual always tries to cure positive social evils, such as wars, by negative individual actions, such as non-co-operation, passive resistance or conscientious objection. This is because he cannot rid himself of the assumption that the individual is free. But we have shown that the individual is never free. He can only attain freedom by social co-operation. He can only do what he wants by using social forces. If, therefore, he wishes to stop poverty, war, and misery, he must do it, not by passive resistance, but by using social relations. But in order to use social relations he must understand them. He must become conscious of the laws of society, just as, if he wants to lever up a stone, he must know the laws of levers.

Once the bourgeois intellectual can see that society is the only instrument of freedom, he has advanced a step farther along the road to freedom. But until then he is unfree. True he is a logician, he understands the causality of nature, Einstein's theories, all the splendid apparatus of social discovery, but he still believes in a magic world of social relations divorced from these theories, in which only the god of bourgeois liberty rules. This is proved, not only in his theory, in the way his doctrine of liberty is accepted like a theological dogma, and never made to square with all his philosophic and scientific knowledge ; but it is also proved in action, when the bourgeois intellectual is powerless to stop the development of increasing unfreedom in bourgeois society. All the compulsions of militancy, fascism, and economic distress harry contemporary society, and all he can oppose to them is individualistic action, conscientious objection and passive resistance. This is bound to be the case if he is unfree. Like a man who believes he can walk upon the water and drowns in it, the bourgeois intellectual asserts a measure of freedom that does not in fact exist, and is therefore unfree mentally and physically. Who cannot see iron compulsion stalking through the bourgeois world to-day ? We are free when we can do what we will. Society is an instrument of freedom in so far as it secures what men want. The members of bourgeois society, all of them, worker, capitalist, and capitalist-intellectual, want an increase in material wealth, happiness, freedom from strife, from danger of death, security. But bourgeois society to-day produces a decrease in material wealth and also creates unemployment, unhappiness, strife, insecurity, constant war. Therefore all who live in bourgeois society—democratic, Fascist or Rooseveltian—are unfree, for bourgeois society is not giving them what they desire. The fact that they have, or have not, votes or 'freedom of speech' does not alter, in any way, their unfreedom.

Why does not bourgeois society fulfil the wants of its members ? Because it does not understand the laws of economic production—it is unorganised and unplanned. It is unconscious of the necessities of economic production, and, because of that, cannot make economic production fulfil its desires. Why is it unconscious of the necessities of economic production? Because, for historical reasons, it believes that economic production is best when each man is left free to produce for himself what seems to him most profitable to produce. In other words, it believes that freedom is secured by the lack of social organisation of the individual in the function of society, economic production. As we saw, this individual freedom through unconsciousness is a delusion. Unconscious, deluded bourgeois society is therefore unfree. Even Russell is unfree; and in the next war, as in the last, will be put in gaol.

This very unfreedom—expressed as individualism—in the basic function of society, ultimately generates every form of external constraint. The bourgeois revolutionary asserted a fallacious liberty—that man was born good and was everywhere in chains, that institutions made him bad. It turned out that this liberty he claimed was individualism in private production. This revealed its fallacious nature as a freedom by appearing at once as a restraint. For it could only be secured, it was only a name, for unrestricted right to own the means of production, which is in itself a restriction on those who are thus alienated from their livelihood. Obviously, what I own absolutely my neighbour is restricted from touching.

All social relations based on duty and privilege were changed by the bourgeois revolution into exclusive and forcible rights to ownership of cash. I produce for my individual self, for profit. Necessarily, therefore, I produce for the market, not for use. I work for cash, not from duty to my lord or retainer. My duties to the State could all now be compounded for cash. All my obligations of contract, whether of marriage or social organisation, could be compounded for cash. Cash appeared as the only obligation between men and men, who were otherwise apparently completely free—free master, free labourer, free producer, free consumer, free markets, free trade, free entrepreneur, the free flow of capital from hand to hand and land to land. And even man's obligations to cash appeared an obligation of cash to him, to be absolutely owned by him.

This dissolution of social obligations could be justified if man was free in himself, and if, doing what seemed best for him, for his own good and profit, he would in fact get what he desired, and so secure freedom. It was a return to the apparent liberty of the jungle, where each beast struggles only for himself, and owes no obligations to anyone. But this liberty, as we saw, is an illusion. The beast is less free than man. The desires of the jungle cancel each other out, and no one gets exactly what he wants. No beast is free.

This fallacy at once revealed itself as a fallacy in the following way. Complete freedom to own property meant that society found itself divided into haves and have-nots, like the beasts in the jungle. The have-nots, each trying to do what was best for him in the given circumstances, according to the bourgeois doctrine of liberty, would have forcibly seized the property from the haves. But this would have been complete anarchy, and though anarchy, according to bourgeois theory, is complete liberty, in practice the bourgeois speedily sees that to live in the jungle is not to be free. Property is the basis of his mode of living. In such circumstances social production could not be carried on, and society would dissolve, man return to savagery, and freedom altogether perish. Thus the bourgeois contradicted his theory in practice from the start. The State took its distinctive modern form as the enforcement of bourgeois rights by coercion. Police, standing army and laws were all brought into being to protect the haves from the 'free' desires of the have-nots. Bourgeois liberty at once gives rise to bourgeois coercion, to prisons, armies, contracts, to all the sticky and restraining apparatus of the law, to all the ideology and education centred round the sanctity of private property, to all the bourgeois commandments. Thus bourgeois liberty was built on a lie, bound to reveal in time its contradictions.

Among the have-nots, bourgeois freedom gave rise to fresh coercions. The free labourer, owning nothing, was free to sell his labour in any market. But this became a form of slavery worse, in its unrestricted form, than chattel slavery, a horror that Government Blue Books describing pre-Factory Act conditions make vivid for all their arid phraseology. They show how unrestricted factory industrialisation made beasts of men, women, and children, how they died of old age in their thirties, how they rose early in the morning exhausted to work and knocked off late at night only to sink exhausted to sleep, how the children were aged by work before they had ceased to be infants. Made worse than a slave—for he was still free to be unemployed—the labourer fought for freedom by enforcing social restraints on his employers. Banding with others in trade unions, he began the long fight that gave rise to the various Factory Acts, wage agreements, and all the elaborate social legislation which to-day coerces the bourgeois employer.

And, after all this, even the bourgeois himself is not free. The unrestricted following of his illusion of liberty enslaves him. His creed demands unrestricted competition, and this, because it is unrestricted, works as wildly and blindly as the weather. It makes him as unfree, as much at the mercy of a not understood chance, as a cork bobbing on the waves. So he too seeks freedom in restraint—industry is increasingly sheltered by amalgamations, rings, tariffs, price agreements, 'unfair competition' clauses, subsidies, and Government protection for the exploitation of Colonial areas. Bourgeois liberty makes overt its self-contradictions by becoming monopoly.

Here is the secret paradox of bourgeois development and decline. The bourgeois abandoned feudal relations in the name of a liberty which he visualised as freedom from social restraints. Such a liberty would have led to savagery. But in fact the liberty he claimed—'unrestricted' private property—really involved restraint, that is, it gave rise to complex forms of social organisation, which were more manysided, more incessant, and more all-pervading, than feudal restraints. Thus the cash relation, which he conceived as putting an end to all social restraints, and thus giving him liberty, did give him a larger measure of liberty than in feudalism, but in the opposite way to his expectations, by imposing far more complex organisations than those of feudal civilisation. All the elaborate forms of bourgeois contracts, market organisation, industrial structure, national States, trade unions, tariffs, Imperialism, and bureaucratic democratic government, the iron pressure of the consumer and the labour market, the dole, subsidy, bounties—all these multifarious forms of social organisation—were brought into being by a class that demanded the dissolution of social organisation. And the fact that bourgeois civilisation obtained a greater measure of control over its environment than feudal—and was that much freer—is precisely because all these complex social organisations were brought into being—but brought blindly.

Blindly brought into being ; that is the source of the ultimate unfreedom of bourgeois civilisation. Because it is not conscious of the fact that private ownership of the means of production, unrestricted competition, and the cash nexus of their natures, involve various forms of restraint—alienation from property, captivity to slump and war, unemployment and misery—bourgeois society is unable to control itself. The various forms of social organisation it has blindly erected, as an animal tunnelling for gold might throw up great mounds of earth, are all haphazard and not understood.

It believes that to become conscious of them fully, to manipulate them consciously for the ends of the will, is to be an advocate of determinism, to kill liberty, to bring into birth the bee-hive state. For still, in spite of all the havoc the bourgeois sees around him, he believes that only the beast is free, and that to be subject to all the winds of chance, at the mercy of wars and slumps and social strife, is to be free.

Any definition of liberty is humbug that does not mean this: liberty to do what one wants. A people is free whose members have liberty to do what they want—to get the goods they desire and avoid the ills they hate. What do men want? They want to be happy, and not to be starved or despised or deprived of the decencies of life. They want to be secure, and friendly with their fellows, and not conscripted to slaughter and be slaughtered. They want to marry, and beget children, and help, not oppress each other. Who is free who cannot do these things, even if he has a vote, and free speech? Who then is free in bourgeois society, for not a few men but millions are forced by circumstances to be unemployed, and miserable, and despised, and unable to enjoy the decencies of life? Millions are forced to go out and be slaughtered, or to kill, and to oppress each other. Millions are forced to strive with their fellows for a few glittering prizes, and to be deprived of marriage, and a home, and children, because society cannot afford them these things. Millions and millions of men are not free. These are the elements of liberty, and it is insane—until these are achieved—for a limited class to believe it can secure the subtleties of liberty. Only when these necessities are achieved, can man rise higher and, by the practice of art and science, learn more clearly what he wants, and what he can get; having only then passed from the sphere of necessity to that of freedom.

Each step to higher consciousness is made actively with struggle and difficulty. It is man's natural but fatal error to suppose that the path of liberty is easy, that is a mere negative, a relaxation, the elimination of an obstacle in his path. But it is more than that. True freedom must be created as strenuously as we make the instruments of freedom, tools and machines. It must be wrested out of the heart of reality, including the inner reality of man's mind.

That is why all lovers of liberty, who have understood the nature of freedom, and escaped from the ignorant categories of bourgeois thought, turn to Communism. For that is simply what Communism is, the attainment of more liberty than bourgeois society can reach. Communism has as its basis the understanding of the causality of society, so that all the unfreedom involved in bourgeois society, the enslavement of the have-nots by the haves, and the slavery of both haves and have-nots to wars, slumps, depression and superstition, may be ended. To be conscious of the laws of dead matter: that is something; but it is not enough. Communism seizes hold of a higher degree of self-determination, to rescue man from war, starvation, hate, and coercion, by becoming conscious of the causality of society. It is Communism that makes free will real to man, by making society conscious of itself. To change reality we must understand its laws. If we *wish* to move a stone, we *must* apply the leverage in the proper place. If we *wish* to change bourgeois social relations into communist, we *must* follow a certain path. The have-nots, the proletariat, must take over the means of production from the haves, the bourgeoisie, and since, as we saw, these two freedoms are incompatible, restraint, in the form of the coercive state, must remain in being as long as the bourgeoisie try to get back their former property. But, unlike the former situation, this stage is only temporary. This stage is what is known as the dictatorship of the proletariat, the necessary step from the dictatorship of the bourgeoisie—which is what the bourgeois state is —to the classless state, which is what Communism is. And as Russia shows, even in the dictatorship of the proletariat, before the classless State has come into being, man is already freer. He can avoid unemployment, and competition with his fellows, and poverty. He can marry and beget children, and achieve the decencies of life. He is not asked to oppress his fellows.

To the worker, subject to unemployment, starved in the midst of plenty, this path eventually becomes plain. Despite the assurances of the bourgeoisie that in a democratic or national State he is completely free, he revolts. And who, in those days, will stand by his side? Will the bourgeoisie, themselves pinched and disfranchised by the growing concentration of capital, discouraged, pessimistic, harried into war and oppression by 'forces beyond control', and yet still demanding liberty? On the answer to that question, which each individual bourgeois must make, sooner or later, will depend whether he strives in those days to make men free or to keep them in chains. And this too depends on whether he has understood the nature of liberty. The class to whom capitalism means liberty steadily contracts, but those once of that class who are now enslaved to war, and imperialism and poverty, still cling to that bourgeois interpretation of liberty that has abundantly proved its falsehood. They can only escape and become free by understanding the active nature of liberty, and by becoming conscious of the path they must follow to attain it. Their will is not free as long as they will liberty but produce unfreedom. It is only free when they will communism and produce liberty.

This good, liberty, contains all good. Not only at the simple level of current material wants, but where all men's aspirations bud, freedom is the same goal, pursued in the same way. Science is the means by which man learns what he can do, and therefore it explores the necessity of outer reality. Art is the means by which man learns what he wants to do, and therefore it explores the essence of the human heart. And bourgeoisdom, shutting its eyes to beauty, turning its back on science, only follows its stupidity to the end. It crucifies liberty upon a cross of gold, and if you ask in whose name it does this, it replies, 'In the name of personal freedom.'